Things That Are Better Than Money

by

John Avanzini

Harrison House
Tulsa, Oklahoma

Things That Are Better Than Money

ISBN: 0-89274-781-1

First Printing: 250,000 copies

Unless otherwise indicated, all Scripture quotations are taken from the *King James Version* of the Bible.

Verses marked **Amplified** are Scripture taken from THE AMPLIFIED BIBLE, Old Testament copyright © 1965, 1987 by The Zondervan Corporation. The Amplified New Testament copyright © 1958, 1987 by The Lockman Foundation. Used by permission.

For emphasis, the author has placed selected words from the Bible quotations in italics.

Harrison House
P.O. Box 35035
Tulsa, OK 74153

Contents

Foreword

The timing of a book's release is as important as its subject. This book by John Avanzini comes at exactly the right time.

I believe the message of faith and prosperity that is in the Church today has been sent by God, because the cost of taking the gospel into all the world is higher in our day than anyone could have ever imagined. No longer are we simply raising a few thousand dollars to purchase some pews and an organ. The Church now faces the necessity of raising millions and millions of dollars to purchase the high-tech communication equipment required for today's mass evangelism.

Add to this the fact that the doors of almost every nation on earth are now open to the gospel, and you will find that millions of dollars will not be enough. It will take billions.

Having bought and paid for nearly 500 television stations, *Trinity Broadcasting Network* understands just how important the message of biblical economics is to the Body of Christ. The saints of God must prosper financially if they are to meet this challenge. Jan and I thank God for the men and women who faithfully teach the biblical message of seed time and harvest. We know it has not been easy for them, for they have been opposed by vicious, self-appointed critics who have openly slandered them, misrepresenting to the Body of Christ what these men and women of God are actually teaching. They have wrongfully accused them of teaching that the Bible primarily talks about money and getting more money. I can personally attest to the fact that teachers of faith do not believe money is the most important thing the Bible teaches.

This book comes as a blessing to all of those who believe the Bible teaches abundance through faith in God's Word. It comes at exactly the right time to set the record straight, for John Avanzini writes of the many things God's Word openly proclaims to be more valuable than mere money.

In closing, I must go one step further and say that after reading the truths so simply stated in *Things That Are Better Than Money,* I came to the same conclusion that Bro. John did. As wonderful and glorious as everything mentioned in this book might be, it still takes money to get its message out to the lost and dying of this world.

The Apostle Paul asked this simple question: **"... how shall they preach except they be sent? . . ."** (Romans 10:15).

The wisest man who ever lived answered this question long before Paul asked it. King Solomon said, **"... money answers all things"** (Ecclesiastes 10:19).

Paul F. Crouch, President
Trinity Broadcasting Network

1

Things Better Than Money

... Thy money perish with thee. ...
Acts 8:20

For over eighteen years, I have dedicated the major portion of my life to teaching biblical economics. During this time I have heard much criticism from those who don't fully understand my teaching. One thing these people say is that I overemphasize the importance of money.

Now please notice they never accuse the leading evangelists of overemphasizing salvation. Neither do they say the teachers of prophecy have too much to say about the Second Coming.

If they would only think, people would understand why I have so much to say about money. The reason is that my boss (God the Father) has assigned me the job of specializing in biblical economics. Since the subject of biblical economics deals primarily with what the Bible says about finances, it only stands to reason that I would have much to say about money!

Just as it would be impossible for the evangelist to preach without primarily explaining that Jesus saves, it would be impossible for me to teach biblical economics without constantly mentioning money.

Satan Is a Bible Student

There is a definite reason for opposition to the message of prosperity in the Body of Christ. Satan knows a rich Church would be much more believable to a lost and dying world than a poor Church. Please note that this statement is not a mere opinion of mine. It is based in biblical fact. The passage of Scripture I am about to share with you thoroughly supports the statement. However, strange as it may seem, most Christians don't even know it exists.

> This wisdom have I seen also under the sun, and it seemed great unto me:
> There was a little city, and few men within it; and there came a great king against it, and besieged it, and built great bulwarks against it:
> Now there was found in it a poor wise man, and he by his wisdom delivered the city; yet no man remembered that same poor man.
> Then said I, Wisdom is better than strength: nevertheless *the poor man's wisdom is despised, and his words are not heard.*
> **Ecclesiastes 9:13-16**

Yes, you are reading correctly. The Scripture boldly states that no one listens to poor people. I am convinced that when he saw these verses, the devil immediately launched an all-out campaign to bring the doctrine of insufficiency into the Church. The devil knew if men taught God's Word of abundance without opposition, prosperity would quickly come to God's children. He also knew that as soon as prosperity came, the Church would be able to fund world evangelism properly. Then everyone would hear a clear witness of the gospel, and multitudes would be saved. As soon as he learned that no one listens to poor people, the devil began to replace the truth of God's abundant supply with the religious tradition of barely getting by.

Ignorance Is Expensive

It is clear that the Church has paid absolutely no attention to the verse that says no one listens to poor people. Why, it's as if the Bible had never even brought forth these words. Instead, just the opposite is true, for there is a church-wide acceptance of the erroneous virtues of shortage and insufficiency. In fact, it goes beyond just accepting the message of insufficiency and poverty. There is organized opposition to the biblically correct message of abundance and prosperity. It seems impossible, but this blindness goes even deeper. The Church has actually formed special, elite, ecclesiastical orders of priests and preachers who take firm vows of poverty. They sincerely believe that taking this unscriptural position will make them and their message more believable.

Oh, Church! When will we wake up from this delusion of the devil? Solomon didn't say everyone listens to the poor man's wisdom. He clearly said "**. . . the poor man's wisdom is . . . not heard**" (Ecclesiastes 9:16).

To give you a small idea of how firmly entrenched the erroneous doctrine of insufficiency is, hear this statistic. I have been teaching biblical economics for almost twenty years. God has given me many breakthroughs — revelations such as the wealth of the wicked that is laid up for the just, and the truth about the debt-canceling power of God. A sizable part of the Church is now accepting both of these truths. However, when it comes to the message of abundance — I mean real abundance, sufficiency to the point that you would have **"... all things that pertain unto life and godliness"** (2 Peter 1:3), and that you would want for absolutely nothing (Psalm 34:10) — sad to say, everyone except the strongest believer in the message of faith, draws back. Instead of the Church using Ecclesiastes 9:16 on the devil, the devil is using it on the Church.

The Power of Misinformation

There is a powerful weapon of warfare. It's a weapon that every successful army throughout history has used. It's called "misinformation."

Satan is using this powerful weapon on the Church of our day, and it is causing destruction in the lives of many of God's children. There is a specific verse of Scripture that can explain this mess. It comes as a word of warning from our God.

> **My people are destroyed for lack of knowledge. . . .**
> **Hosea 4:6**

The misinformation the devil puts out about Scripture thrives where people lack knowledge of God's Word.

Why Traditions Prevail

The main reason unscriptural traditions about poverty remain in the Church is that the children of God *don't study their Bibles enough to recognize misinformation when they hear it.* If we would only do as the Scripture teaches and study to show ourselves approved, the Church of our day would not be standing before a dying world at the end of time, empty-handed.

Hear this statement and hear it well. We must get back to the study of God's Word.

> **Study to show thyself approved unto God, *a workman that needeth not to be ashamed,* rightly dividing the word of truth.**
> **2 Timothy 2:15**

Victory Is Coming

Please don't despair! Victory is on the horizon, for the Bible says the end of men's traditions is now at hand. Simon Peter prophesied that restoration would come just before our Lord returns. Hear the bold promise he made to those of us who have the privilege of living at the end of the age.

> **Repent ye therefore, and be converted, that your sins may be blotted out, when the times of refreshing shall come from the presence of the Lord;**
> **And he shall send *Jesus Christ,* which before was preached unto you:**
> **Whom the *heaven must receive until the times of restitution of all things, which God hath spoken by the mouth of all his holy prophets since the world began.***
> **Acts 3:19-21**

What a wonderful promise! The apostle says restoration is coming to the Church in the last days. Here is the best part. This promise is for us, for we are those saints who live in the last days of time.

Better Than Money

The Bible is, without a doubt, the most complete book in existence. It deals with marriage, rearing children, honesty, rebellion, prophecy, salvation, heaven, and hell, as well as many other subjects. Upon close observation it becomes obvious that the Bible deals primarily with practical things. The reason it has much to say about money is that financial matters are practical matters. However, let me quickly add something even more significant. Nowhere does Scripture ever say that money is the most important thing.

In the following pages, I will bring to you from God's Word a number of wonderful things that are much better than money. (Please note: They do not appear in order of their value or importance.) I hope they will bless you as much as they have blessed me and that they will help bring balance to your understanding of God's plan of abundance for you and His Church.

2

Your Good Name

If you were to ask a group of people to write down the ten most valuable things they own, few, if any, would place a *good name* on the list. However, the Word of God tells us that a good name is one of the most valuable things a person can have. The Bible lists it as one of those special things that is more precious than money.

> **A good name is rather to be chosen than great riches. . . .**
> **Proverbs 22:1**

King Solomon was so much impressed with the benefit of having a good name, he declared it to be more valuable than monetary standards could measure. Upon examination, you will be even more impressed with the importance Solomon placed on a good name, for he made another statement about its value in the Book of Ecclesiastes.

> **A good name is better than precious ointment; and the day of death than the day of one's birth.**
> **Ecclesiastes 7:1**

In this verse, Solomon says that a good name has a better effect on a man's dignity during his lifetime than the effect embalming ointment has on his body after death. In other words, Solomon says a good name preserves a man better in life than embalming oils do in death.

Entering Heaven

The Book of Psalms powerfully describes the benefits of having a good name. While the words *good name* do not actually appear, the following verse is clearly a description of a man who has one.

> **Lord, who may go and find refuge and shelter in your tabernacle up on your holy hill?**
> **Psalm 15:1, TLB**

In so many words, the psalmist is asking what kind of person God is going to allow in heaven. In the next few verses, God gives a powerful answer. I ask you to notice that His answer is totally different from the answer of many religious leaders of our day. The Lord describes the man He will allow to spend eternity in His heaven as one of integrity and honor, a person with a *good name,* if you please.

> **Anyone who *leads a blameless life* and *is truly sincere.* Anyone who *refuses to slander others, does not listen to gossip, never harms his neighbor, speaks out against sin, criticizes those committing it, commends the faithful followers of the Lord, keeps a promise even if it ruins him, does not crush his debtors with high interest rates,* and *refuses to testify against the innocent despite the bribes offered him*—such a man shall stand firm forever.**
> **Psalm 15:2-5, TLB**

I Almost Lost My Good Name

The value of my good name is an ever-present reality to me. The reason is that there was a day when someone took my good name from me. It looked as if I had lost it forever. I must now tell you of a most horrible season of my life. It was when my wife and I had to fight a legal battle to clear my good name. The dishonest dealings of some business associates brought this nightmare into our lives. Their dark deeds almost cost us everything we had. In fact, this experience did cost us every material possession we owned. We literally spent all our money. We even lost our home and both of our cars. However, we gave them up willingly, because when you are in a battle for your good name, you quickly realize that the Bible is correct when it says a good name is more precious than great riches. We gladly gave up the things of lesser value (our material riches) to regain that which is without price, our good name.

We thank God daily for the knowledge He has given us in biblical economics. Since those awful days of losing everything, we have been able to replace all the material possessions we lost, by properly applying the knowledge of His Word as to giving and receiving. I am convinced that few people will ever fully realize how important their good name is, that is, until they lose it.

Abraham Valued His Good Name

Abraham's good name was of the utmost importance to him. The Bible tells us he refused the mega-wealth of two prominent eastern cities (Sodom and Gomorrah), rather than have his good name associated with the base practices of the Sodomites of his day. If you remember, the king of Sodom offered Abraham all the wealth of Sodom and Gomorrah as a reward for delivering Abraham's nephew, Lot, and the other people of Sodom from the hand of the invading kings.

> **And the king of Sodom said unto Abram, Give me the persons, and take *the goods to thyself.***
> **And Abram said to the king of Sodom, I have lift up mine hand unto the Lord, the most high God . . .**
> **. . . that I will not take any thing *that is thine, lest thou [the king of Sodom] shouldest say, I have made Abram rich.***
> **Genesis 14:21-23**

Obviously Abraham felt that no amount of money was worth the smearing of his good name. God's Word clearly documents that Father Abraham believed his good name to be more valuable than all the riches of the two most wicked cities of his day.

Joseph Valued His Good Name

The Word of God brings forth another tremendous illustration of the importance of having a good name. It comes to us from the life of a young man named Joseph. Scripture tells us that during his early years in Egypt, he was temporarily elevated to the position of chief steward over the house of an important businessman named Potiphar.

During his time of service there, his master's wife constantly attempted to seduce him. How easy it would have been for Joseph to have gone along with her advances. If he would only have compromised, no doubt he would have come into favor with the lady of the house. However, Joseph counted his good name more valuable than the favor of man or woman.

> One day at about this time Potiphar's wife began making eyes at Joseph, and suggested that he come and sleep with her.
>
> Joseph refused. "Look," he told her, "my master trusts me with everything in the entire household; he himself has no more authority here than I have! He has held back nothing from me except you yourself because you are his wife. How can I do such a wicked thing as this? It would be a great sin against God."
>
> But she kept on with her suggestions day after day, even though he refused to listen, and kept out of her way as much as possible. Then one day as he was in the house going about his work — as it happened, *no one else was around at the time* — she came and grabbed him by the sleeve demanding, "Sleep with me." He tore himself away, but as he did, his jacket slipped off and she was left holding it as he fled from the house.
>
> **Genesis 39:7-12, TLB**

Even though Potiphar's wife insisted, Joseph didn't give in and compromise. His righteous reaction to her advances caused her to lie about what actually happened. Because of her false testimony, Joseph ended up in prison.

Some might say Joseph's acts of righteousness didn't save his good name. They actually ruined it. His integrity caused him to go to prison for attempted rape. Please know this truth. It is desirable to have a good name with men, but above all else, *it is imperative that you have a good name with God.* Joseph knew it was better to face ruin before men and spend his life in jail, than to lose his good name with God and risk facing eternity in hell. Hear his words to Potiphar's wife as she reached out to grab him.

> ". . . How can I do such a wicked thing as this? *It would be a great sin against God.*"
> **Genesis 39:9, TLB**

Everyone in Egypt might have believed the woman's story. However, God knew that Joseph had not sinned against Him. Joseph did what few men would have done. He kept his good name with his God.

I have a favorite saying about a good name. It goes like this: The true measure of a man is not determined by what he does before men, but by what he does when no one will ever know what he did.

Thank God, there was more to Joseph than just trying to get ahead. He also had the integrity not to sin against his God.

In this chapter, I believe I have shown you one of many things more valuable than mere money. It's a good name!

3

A Good Spouse

... they shall be one flesh.
Genesis 2:24

I never hear the word *spouse* without thinking of the good wife God has given me. Surely she has proved much more valuable than mere money. I agree with the thirty-first chapter of Proverbs when it says:

Who can find a virtuous woman? for her price is far above rubies.
Proverbs 31:10

A Forceful Woman

God most surely gave me one of those rare treasures, for I have a virtuous woman as a wife. Let me now bring to your attention how easy it is to miss the true meaning of this verse. The King James writers weakly interpreted one of the original words of this verse. I speak of the word *virtuous*. In the Hebrew it is the word *chayil*. Its actual meaning is stronger than just the word *virtuous*. According to Strong's concordance,* it means "a force, whether of men, means, or other resources; an army, wealth, virtue, valor, or strength." With that definition in mind, the verse

---

*   *James Strong, The Exhaustive Concordance of the Bible*
     (Methodist Book Concern, New York, 1923)

takes on an expanded meaning. Following is a better translation: Who can find a forceful, resourceful, strong woman, one who is full of virtue and valor; for her value is far above rubies.

A Rare Treasure

As you read through Proverbs 31, notice that the man who has this type of wife is safe with her and can trust confidently in her. Her activities bring forth multiple benefits to him throughout all the years of his life. You will find that the virtuous wife is a willing worker. She is not afraid of some of the four-letter words that many of the women of our day hate to hear—words such as *work, iron, cook, bake, wash,* and *dust.*

The virtuous woman also has a good mind for business. She is definitely not the helpless, airhead type. She becomes involved in the financial decisions of the home and business. You won't hear her say, "I just don't understand anything about money matters."

She considereth a field, and buyeth it: with the fruit of her hands she planteth a vineyard.
Proverbs 31:16

She is generous to the poor (31:20). Who is more qualified to teach concern for the underprivileged than a compassionate mother and wife?

The Blood of Jesus Covers Her House

It is interesting to note how clearly the King James Version draws a picture of household salvation in verse 21. It speaks of this virtuous woman as having no fear of the snow for her household. In the snowy season everything looks as if it has died. It is a perfect picture of death. The reason she doesn't fear the death angel is that her family is covered in scarlet. Scarlet is the universal picture of the saving blood of Jesus.

Thank God for godly mothers who keep the gospel of Jesus ever before their households. Hear the writer of Proverbs as he so aptly describes this dimension of the virtuous woman's activities.

> **She is not afraid of the snow for her household: for all her household are clothed with scarlet.**
> **Proverbs 31:21**

An Elder's Wife

One of the benefits she brings her husband is that her stability and good sense cause him to rise into leadership in God's house, as well as in the community. He sits as an elder in the gate (31:23).

A quick reading of the power-packed words of this chapter in its entirety will quickly settle the matter. A good wife is much more valuable than mere money.

The Wicked Don't Know

Many men don't know the value of a good wife. On a recent television special, I heard one of the best-known citizens of New York City. If I said his name, you would immediately recognize it. In the interview, he made the statement that his money was much more important to him than either his wife or his girlfriend.

This man used to be a billionaire empire builder and casino owner. Notice that I said, used to be. Yes, that's right. This so-called "wonder boy, jet-setter" is now bankrupt. It's interesting to watch the foolish big shots of the world system, those whose lives so strongly contradict the Word of God. No matter how famous and wealthy they become or how happy they seem, God always has the last laugh.

> **He that sitteth in the heavens shall laugh:**
> **the Lord shall have them in derision.**
> **Psalm 2:4**

Warning About the Wrong Wife

The Word of God carries a warning about choosing a shameful wife. The writer of Proverbs shows us how unfavorably she compares to the virtuous woman.

> **A virtuous woman is a crown to her**
> **husband: but she that maketh ashamed is as**
> **rottenness in his bones.**
> **Proverbs 12:4**

How descriptive this verse is! The virtuous woman is a crown to her husband. The man married to her will feel like a king. However, the shameful wife will bring a man to disgrace, and her husband will feel as if termites and dry rot have taken over his bones.

The Bible also speaks of the horror of living with a contentious woman.

> **It is better to dwell in the wilderness, than**
> **with a contentious and an angry woman.**
> **Proverbs 21:19**

A Good Husband

In the same way, there is tremendous value in finding a good husband, for he also is more valuable than rubies or riches. Please note that I am not speaking of a good husband by the standards of the world. I am speaking of the man who fulfills God's qualifications for being a good husband. The Book of Ephesians outlines them for us.

> **Husbands, love your wives, even as Christ also loved the church, and gave himself for it;**
> **So ought men to love their wives as their own bodies. He that loveth his wife loveth himself.**
> **For no man ever yet hated his own flesh; but nourisheth and cherisheth it, even as the Lord the church.**
> **Ephesians 5:25,28,29**

A God-approved husband loves his wife in the same way Jesus loves the Church. Just as Jesus gladly laid down His life for the Church, a godly husband will always be ready to lay down his life for his wife. He will also be constantly helping his wife to grow from one glory in Christ to the next, until she finally comes forth in the marvelous image of Jesus Christ Himself.

> **But we all, with open face beholding as in a glass the glory of the Lord, are changed into the same image from glory to glory, even as by the Spirit of the Lord.**
> **2 Corinthians 3:18**

Like His Own Flesh

The God-approved husband loves his wife, even as he loves himself. He is never hateful nor rude toward her.

Instead he is constantly nurturing and cherishing her, even preferring her as Jesus prefers the Church. This kind of husband will look upon his wife as a bride all the days of their marriage. He will never refer to her as his "old lady," "the war department," or any other demeaning title.

Warning About the Wrong Husband

The Scriptures also speak about the terrors of marrying the wrong husband.

As coals are to burning coals, and wood to fire; so is a contentious man to kindle strife.
Proverbs 26:21

God help the woman who marries a man because he is handsome, popular, or wealthy. She will be infinitely better off marrying a plain man who will treat her as Jesus does. The qualities of a godly husband will long outlast the good looks, popularity, or money of the playboy type.

The Bible also tells us that a proper husband will diligently work to provide for his family. It goes on to tell us that an able-bodied man who does not provide a living for his own family is worse than an infidel.

But if any provide not for his own, and specially for those of his own house, he hath denied the faith, and is worse than an infidel.
1 Timothy 5:8

With these few scriptural qualifications in mind, I hope it has become evident that a good spouse is much better than any amount of money could ever be.

4

The Word of God

How sweet are thy words. . . .
Psalm 119:103

The quality of life in any society rises and falls in direct proportion to how important the Word of God is to its people and their leaders. All moral law and social justice find their basis in the Book we call "the Holy Bible." It has guided kings, generals, presidents, ambassadors, mothers and fathers, as well as their children. It brings conviction into the hearts of the basest of men, as well as to those we consider above reproach.

An Instant Best-Seller

Without question, the Bible is the greatest book ever written. History tells us it was the first book printed on the first printing press. Since that day, not one year has passed without its being a best-seller.

Tyrants have burned it; rulers have banned it. However, it has never gone out of existence. Theologians have debated it, liberals have tried to dilute it, and scoffers have ridiculed it. Still it stands stronger than ever. In recent years, an entire society attempted to outlaw it, only to emerge from behind its iron wall of atheism with a population hungering and thirsting for the Word of God.

Anvils and Hammers

The following illustration has always been special to me. It is about a blacksmith who had saved every hammer he had ever worn out during his long career. He kept the old, battered hammers in a stack in the corner of his shop. People often made comments about the stack of discarded hammers. Occasionally someone would ask how many anvils the hammers had worn out. The answer always seemed to surprise everyone. The blacksmith would reply, "I have had only one anvil since I opened this business. It's still sitting here in the middle of the shop, waiting to wear out the next hammer that comes against it."

What a good parable this story makes about the durability of God's Word. The anvil portrays the Bible, and the worn out hammers are a perfect example of the foolish men who have dared to come against it. In the same way that the blacksmith wore out and threw all the hammers to one side, so the opponents of God's Word eventually end up broken and discarded. The Word of God, as the anvil, steadfastly resists every blow without showing any wear.

The Psalmist minces no words when he tells us God's Word is more valuable than money.

The law of [God's] mouth is better unto me
than thousands of gold and silver.
Psalm 119:72

Faith Comes by the Word of God

Without faith it is impossible to have any kind of meaningful relationship with God. The Word of God is clear.

> **But without faith it is impossible to please [God]. . . .**
>
> **Hebrews 11:6**

How emphatic these words are! It is absolutely impossible to please God without faith.

God's Word tells us that faith comes by hearing the Word of God.

> **So then faith cometh by hearing, and hearing by the word of God.**
>
> **Romans 10:17**

The Word of God is the giver of faith, thereby making it of infinite value, for **"without faith it is impossible to please him. . ."** (Hebrews 11:6).

More Valuable Than Riches

Hear King David as he tells of the value of God's Word.

> **God's laws are perfect. They protect us, make us wise, and give us joy and light. God's laws are pure, eternal, just. They are more desirable than *gold*. They are sweeter than honey dripping from a honeycomb. For they warn us away from harm and give success to those who obey them.**
>
> **Psalm 19:7-11, TLB**

A Guide

The Word of God has always been ready to guide those who are open to instruction. King David tells us it is a precious lamp unto our feet.

Thy word is a lamp unto my feet, and a light unto my path.
Psalm 119:105

It has always been there to bring honorable men and women into a more noble lifestyle.

God gives us His precious Word as a teacher to bring us into perfect understanding of His purposes.

All scripture is given by inspiration of God, and is profitable for doctrine, for reproof, for correction, for instruction in righteousness:
That the man of God may be perfect, throughly furnished unto all good works.
2 Timothy 3:16,17

The Word of God has always been the best guide to keep the souls of men on course with God. It is the best insulation against the contamination of sin for those who hide it in their hearts.

Thy word have I hid in mine heart, that I might not sin against thee.
Psalm 119:11

Only a fool would dare to argue with the fact that the Word of God is one of those wonderful things that is more precious than money.

5

Understanding

. . . with all thy getting get understanding.
Proverbs 4:7

When discussing the things that are more valuable than money, we must include understanding. God's Word is clear about the connection between understanding and being successful in this life. The reason is obvious, for the Bible says with proper understanding comes every other thing you desire. The Book of Proverbs goes even further and says those who take the time to get understanding will have riches and honor, as well as extended life.

> Happy is the man that findeth wisdom, and the man that getteth understanding.
>
> For the merchandise of it is *better than* the merchandise of *silver,* and the gain thereof than *fine gold.*
>
> She is *more precious* than *rubies:* and all the things thou canst desire are not to be compared unto her.
>
> *Length of days* is in her right hand; and in her left hand *riches* and *honor.*
>
> **Proverbs 3:13-16**

Wisdom and Understanding Differ

At first glance, verse 13 seems to be saying that both wisdom and understanding are more valuable than gold and silver. However, upon close examination of the context, you will find that the writer is placing the greater value on understanding. Notice that when he states its worth, he speaks in the singular.

> **For the merchandise of *it* [singular] is better than the merchandise of silver, and the gain thereof than fine gold.**
> **Proverbs 3:14**

It is important to note that wisdom and understanding are not the same. Wisdom is knowing what to do with the knowledge you have. Understanding is something quite different. It is knowing *why* and *how* things happen.

Reason or Revelation

It is necessary to know how understanding comes before you can fully appreciate the importance God places upon it.

There are two very different ways to receive the knowledge that brings understanding. One is by *reason,* and the other is by *revelation.*

REASON: This is the way natural man finds things out. Please know that I would never make light of this way of gathering information, for *the human creature has accomplished tremendous understanding through reason.* Mankind has achieved astonishing progress in the natural realm. For instance, the entire industrial revolution has come to pass through his ability to reason. It has enabled him to do truly marvelous things. However, no matter how impressive this process might be, we must be careful not to think too highly of it. I say this because reason has definite limitations.

REVELATION: There is another method of increasing understanding that is far superior to reasoning. It is limitless in the scope of its knowledge. However, revelation has limitations as to who can use it. Not all men are capable of receiving revelation. It can come only to those who have been born again. When I say born again, I am speaking of those whom God has made spiritually alive. He limits it to this group because revelation knowledge comes only from God the Father, and He is a spirit.

> **God is a *Spirit:* and they that worship him *must* worship him in *spirit* and in truth.**
> **John 4:24**

The spirit of man acquires knowledge from the Spirit of God by the process of revelation. Revelation knowledge brings information to man he cannot obtain any other way. The Apostle Paul makes it clear that the power of reason cannot penetrate the realm of God's knowledge.

> **O the depth of the riches both of the wisdom and knowledge of God! how unsearchable are his judgments, and *his ways past finding out!***
> **Romans 11:33**

Paul says the knowledge of God is in a realm that goes beyond investigation, or reason. "**. . . His ways [are] past finding out!**"

Not by the Five Senses

The following verse should begin to show the importance of revelation.

> **But as it is written,** *Eye* **hath not seen, nor** *ear* **heard, neither have entered into the** *heart* **of man, the things which God hath prepared for them that love him.**
>
> **1 Corinthians 2:9**

In the above verse, the apostle describes the inability of man's reasoning power to discover the things God has prepared for those who love Him. It is well known that the natural, investigative devices of humans are their five senses (seeing, hearing, tasting, smelling, and touching). By these senses, mankind has made all physical discoveries. In 1 Corinthians 2:9, the apostle mentions two of these senses. He says *hearing* and *seeing* cannot discover God's plans for those who love Him.

Then he says the heart of natural man is also useless in finding out God's plans for His children. The word *heart* as it appears here actually means something more than the blood pump that beats within the chest of man. In its biblical sense, it means "the thoughts (thinking process), feelings, emotions, and mind of an individual." I hope you are beginning to see what Paul is saying. He is telling us the mind (soul) of man with its reasoning power, *cannot* find out the things God has planned.

By Revelation

Then the apostle goes on to tell us the method God uses for getting His information to those who communicate with Him. He states that the things He wants us to understand will come to us by a supernatural process He calls "revelation."

> **But God hath *revealed* them unto us by his**
> **Spirit. . . .**
> **1 Corinthians 2:10**

Paul brings this matter to a head in the sixteenth verse when he asks who has understood the mind or thoughts of God. Surely the natural man has not. However, the redeemed of the Lord are different, for they have been born again and have access to the mind (understanding) of Christ.

> **For who hath known the mind of the Lord,**
> **that he may instruct him? But we [the**
> **redeemed] have the mind of Christ.**
> **1 Corinthians 2:16**

Revelation Knowledge

The wonderful aspect of this limitless process called "revelation" is that it is available to all who have come into a personal relationship with our Lord and Savior Jesus Christ. The Apostle Paul specifically prayed that the ability to receive revelation would come upon all of God's children. Yes, that means you.

> **That the God of our Lord Jesus Christ, the**
> **Father of glory, *may give unto you* the spirit of**
> **wisdom and *revelation* in the knowledge of him.**
> **Ephesians 1:17**

Paul specifically asks that revelation would come to you. He further prays that wisdom would also be yours. Remember, wisdom is knowing what to do with the information you receive. Praise God!

Understanding the things of God by revelation is infinitely more valuable than mere money. I know this to be true, for everything I have and everything I have become since I was born again is a direct result of the knowledge I have received from God through revelation. I can honestly say I would not take all the wealth of this world in exchange for the understanding God has given me by revelation. It has safely brought me this far, and it will take me all the way into God's heaven when I die.

Hear with me one more time how truly valuable this ability to understand really is.

> **If thou seekest her as silver, and searchest for her as for hid treasures;**
> **Then shalt thou understand the fear of the Lord, and find the knowledge of God.**
> **Proverbs 2:4,5**

Notice that understanding will not just drop out of the sky on you the day you accept Christ. You must diligently seek after it as if you were looking for silver and hidden treasure. We also receive a large part of revelation by simply asking for it. Now notice I didn't say it comes from asking men. It comes from asking God.

> **Ask, and it shall be given you; seek, and ye shall find; knock, and it shall be opened unto you.**
> **Matthew 7:7**

Understanding God is understanding everything. It is worth far more than the treasures of this world!

6

Being the Temple of God

. . . ye are the temple of the living God. . . .
2 Corinthians 6:16

In the Book of Matthew, Jesus spoke some words to the Pharisees that should have caused a fist fight. Notice the sharpness of His comments.

> Woe unto you, ye blind guides, which say, Whosoever shall swear by the temple, it is nothing; but whosoever shall swear by the gold of the temple, he is a debtor!
>
> Ye fools and blind: for *whether is greater, the gold, or the temple that sanctifieth the gold?*
>
> And, Whosoever shall swear by the altar, it is nothing; but whosoever sweareth by the gift that is upon it, he is guilty.
>
> Ye fools and blind: for whether is greater, the gift, or the altar that sanctifieth the gift?
>
> **Matthew 23:16-19**

With those few words, our Lord let the Pharisees know that the place God calls His temple is infinitely more valuable than the gold that adorns it. He tells them that when they bring their money to the temple, the altar actually has the ability to sanctify the money. The money does not give worth to the altar, but the altar increases the value of the money offered upon it.

You Are the Temple

As often as I have read these choice verses in Matthew 23, I never really grasped the depth of revelation they held. It wasn't until I began to write this book that they became *living truth* to me. When you add these verses to the fact that present-day saints are the *temple of God,* revelation knowledge begins to operate.

> **Know ye not that** *ye are the temple of God,* **and that the Spirit of God dwelleth in you?**
> **If any man defile the temple of God, him shall God destroy; for the temple of God is holy,** *which temple ye are.*
> 1 Corinthians 3:16,17

Open your spirit and think about what these two verses are saying. Matthew tells us the temple of God has the power to sanctify money. Now allow your spirit to take one more step, and realize that we, the born again, are the temple of God. When you merge these two pieces of information together, the revelatory process begins to operate. The redeemed saints of God are more valuable than any amount of money. The children of God are so superior to mere money that when it comes into *proper contact* with them, the value of the money increases. It becomes sanctified money. This thought becomes even more powerful when you realize that the Greek word translated *sanctifieth* (Matthew 23:17) is *hagiazo* which, according to Strong's concordance, means "to make holy, purify, consecrate, or to venerate."

Now hold on to your hat as I merge one more scriptural truth with these two verses. In the Book of Luke,

Jesus asks a question that up to this time no one had answered. Hear it with ears that understand.

> **If therefore ye have not been faithful in the unrighteous mammon, who will commit to your trust the true *riches*?**
> **Luke 16:11**

Italics Speak

Now pay close attention, for the King James Version gives us some special insight into the original language. Upon close examination, you will find that the word *riches* is in italics. When the King James Version italicizes a word, it means the word does not appear in the original text. The translators have added it. Don't just take my word for it. Check it out for yourself. Strong's concordance doesn't assign it a number, nor do any of the interlinear translations acknowledge it in the original text.

Let's paraphrase Luke 16:11 and see what it says if it omits the word *riches:* If you are not faithful with unrighteous money, who will commit to your trust the responsibility of making it into true (money)?

If you are not faithful to do what God has trusted you to do with the unrighteous money of the world system that comes into your control, it can never become *true money*.

If you will notice, this is not a wild idea. The overall context of these verses has to do with being faithful over that which is another man's, for the very next verse says:

> **. . . if ye have not been faithful in that which is another man's, who shall give you that which is your own?**
>
> **Luke 16:12**

The Tithe

With this verse in mind, let's turn our thoughts to God's clear instruction about the tenth of all the money that comes into our possession. God calls it "the tithe." His Word is clear. Ten cents out of every dollar belong to the Lord. They do not belong to us.

> **And all the tithe of the land, whether of the seed of the land, or of the fruit of the tree, is the Lord's: it is holy unto the Lord.**
>
> **And if a man will at all redeem ought of his tithes, he shall add thereto the fifth part thereof.**
>
> **Leviticus 27:30,31**

I am thoroughly convinced that when Christians gain financial increase by their activities in the world system, the money they obtain is tainted money. The Scripture calls it "unrighteous mammon." However, when Christians faithfully tithe on the unrighteous mammon they receive, they sanctify the money. As Luke 16:11 implies, they turn it into true money.

Obedient Saints

Now please notice that the saint of God sanctifies the money only if he does what God has trusted him to do with his money. Remember, God trusts us with the unrighteous money of this world system, so we can turn it into true money.

If therefore ye have not been faithful in the unrighteous mammon, who will commit to your trust the true riches?
Luke 16:11

This is a good time to remember that the word *sanctifieth* (which we saw earlier in this chapter) actually means to "consecrate the money, or make it good and pure again."

. . . for whether is greater, the gold, or the temple that *sanctifieth* the gold?
Matthew 23:17

You Cannot Love Tithed-on Money

It is common knowledge that the servants of the world system love money. However, when you faithfully tithe on the unrighteous mammon you receive from this world, you show to all that you do not love the money. Your obedience in tithing goes even further, for it sanctifies the tainted money of this world by making it the true money of the Kingdom of God.

Now remember, Christians have the power to sanctify money because they are the temple of God. When the tainted gold (money) of this world system comes into a true believer's control, that encounter sanctifies it. When I say true believer, I speak of one who is faithful to tithe on all his income.

Marked Money

Let me add just one more wonderful truth to this chapter. You no doubt know the tithe is 10 percent. When you tithe on your increase, you are clipping 10 percent off your money. In type, you are actually performing *a spiritual ordinance,* for you are *circumcising* your money. In the same way that circumcision marked Israel as a people set apart exclusively for Jehovah's use, the same thing takes place with your money when you tithe from it. Tithing marks it as sanctified and set aside for the Master's use. It actually becomes Kingdom money, or better said, true riches. See it as it really is in the spirit world. In tithing, the person who earns the money brings it to the altar, and causes it to bow the knee before Jehovah God.

God built a tremendous safety factor into the act of tithing, for you will never be able to worship something you have seen bowing the knee to God. You will never be able to worship any money you have tithed on at the altar, no matter how much it might be. In tithing, you cause your money to acknowledge that Jehovah, and Jehovah alone, is God.

I must include you, the modern-day temple of God, on the list of things more valuable than money, for you have the power to sanctify money. Jesus says you do in Matthew 23:16-19.

> **Ye fools and blind: for whether is greater,**
> **the gold, or the temple that sanctifieth the gold?**
> **Matthew 23:17**
> **... ye are the temple of God. ...**
> **1 Corinthians 3:16**

7

The Trying of Your Faith

> . . . the trial of your faith, being much more
> precious than of gold. . . .
> 1 Peter 1:7

The Bible minces no words about the tremendous value of the trying of your faith. If it weren't so clearly stated, it would be easy to miss the value God places upon this process. Hear the apostle as he tells of the infinite profit that comes to us when God tries our faith. He says these most unpleasant experiences are like the refiner's fire that purifies the finest gold.

> . . . the trial of your faith, being much more
> precious than of gold that perisheth, though it be
> tried with fire. . . .
> 1 Peter 1:7

Fiery Trials

I must admit that when I first started writing this chapter, I had to take a deep breath. Like the Apostle Peter, when I think of the opposition of Satan, I tend to think of a series of fiery events instead of precious experiences.

> Beloved, think it not strange concerning the
> fiery trial which is to try you. . . .
> 1 Peter 4:12

It is interesting that Simon Peter calls the times of testing both *precious* (1 Peter 1:7) and *fiery* (1 Peter 4:12). The only explanation is that the actual testing of our faith is like walking through a fire that stands between us and the thing of value that lies on the other side. No one would ever describe the tribulations the saints walk through as fun-filled events. When the devil attacks and tries to overthrow our faith, I'll be the first to admit that it's hard to find any joy in it. However, every victorious Christian knows the following fact. When you have won the battle, and you see the full manifestation of the thing you had hoped for, the fiery fight you had to go through to get it, always becomes one of those profitable experiences. You wouldn't trade it for any amount of money.

The following verse of Scripture describes the fiery trial that precedes a great victory.

> . . . weeping may endure for a night, but joy
> cometh in the morning.
>
> **Psalm 30:5**

Overcomers Must Overcome

My good wife, Patricia, puts it this way: You will never be an overcomer unless you have some things to overcome. Yet a trial can go even deeper, for the trying or testing of a Christian's faith brings forth more than just a victory. After you have won victory after victory and have overcome trial after trial, powerful weapons begin to grow within you. Hear the Apostle Paul as he tells of them.

> . . . we glory in tribulations also: knowing
> that tribulation worketh *patience;*

And patience, *experience;* and experience, *hope:*

And hope *maketh not ashamed;* because the love of God is shed abroad in our hearts by the Holy Ghost which is given unto us.

Romans 5:3-5

Patience

The first byproduct of tribulation is *patience.* Strong's concordance tells us that the word translated *patience* means "cheerful (or hopeful) endurance, constancy." One result of the successful testing of your faith is the development of constancy and endurance. Notice it won't be the worldly kind of endurance — just grinning and bearing it. No, godly endurance always couples with it the virtue of *cheerfulness.* I have actually heard the people of the world say it shows them the true power of God when they see how happy some Christians are, even when everything seems to be going wrong.

Notice how important patience, or constancy, is to receiving from God. James says the man without constancy cannot receive from God.

. . . let him ask in faith, nothing wavering. For he that wavereth is like a wave of the sea driven with the wind and tossed.

For let not that man think that he shall receive any thing of the Lord.

James 1:6,7

Experience

The next benefit that comes from the trying of your faith is *experience.* I like to explain this special asset as *proof.* Here is how it works. First, you stand in faith, believing God to give you something He has promised, even if it looks as if you will never have it. Then, when it does come to pass, you have experienced God's faithfulness. The promise has materialized. You have it in your possession. The manifestation of the thing becomes proof positive that your faith in God's promises works.

David used his past experiences in his victory over Goliath. If you will remember, King Saul tried to talk him out of fighting the giant. However, David remembered some events from his past that made him stand fast. They assured him of God's ability to manifest the victory over the Philistine.

> . . . David said unto Saul, Thy servant kept his father's sheep, and there came a lion, and a bear, and took a lamb out of the flock:
> And I went out after him, and smote him, and delivered it out of his mouth: and when he arose against me, I caught him by his beard, and smote him, and slew him.
> Thy servant slew both the lion and the bear: and this uncircumcised Philistine shall be as one of them, seeing he hath defied the armies of the living God.
> David said moreover, *The Lord that delivered me* out of the paw of the lion, and out of the paw of the bear, *he will deliver me* out of the hand of this Philistine. . . .
>
> **1 Samuel 17:34-37**

I hope you can see the value of past victories. Your faithful stand on God's Word has manifested victories in past battles, and they are proof positive that He has delivered you before. If He did it before, He will most certainly do it again. You know He will, because He is the God who never changes.

> **Jesus Christ the same yesterday, and to day, and for ever.**
> **Hebrews 13:8**

Hope

The next thing that comes to us through the successful outcome of the trying of our faith is hope. Please don't let the popular definition of hope cause you to miss its value. The hope that comes from the trying of your faith is not, as the world thinks it is, *a mere wish*. I am sure you have heard folks say, "I hope everything turns out okay," meaning they are wishing it will turn out all right. That's not biblical hope.

Hear the word *hope* in its true biblical context.

> **And our hope of you [Corinthians] is** *steadfast, knowing [seeing it as done],* **that as ye are partakers of the sufferings [tribulation], so shall ye be also of the consolation [comfort].**
> **2 Corinthians 1:7**

Paul says the hope we have is steadfast, the kind that knows that it knows that God will do what He has promised.

Not Ashamed

Now here is the best part. Hope (seeing what God promised as being already done) brings forth a confidence that is devastating to the devil. Going through the fiery testing of your faith releases a powerful byproduct to your character. It gives you the knowledge that you will never be ashamed for doing what God says nor for believing for anything He has promised you. If the victory has come through one fiery trial after another, you become convinced that trusting God will never embarrass you. When God says a thing is yours, and you believe it by faith, you will never experience embarrassment nor shame by its not coming into manifestation. You can always stand in faith with full confidence, believing God will deliver.

Four Powerful Virtues

When the trying of your faith is complete, you will come forth with the following virtues:

Patience—You will consistently stand without wavering.

Experience—You will have past victories to remember while you wait for even greater victories.

Hope—You will see the things God has promised you as already being done.

No Shame—You will have confidence that standing for God will never embarrass you, for you know God will deliver on His promises.

Surely these virtuous byproducts that come from the fiery trials make the trying of your faith infinitely more valuable than mere money.

8

Strategic Relationships

... Is it a time to receive money? ...
2 Kings 5:26

God places high importance on relationships, especially those that have potential to cause a breakthrough. After being in the ministry over thirty years, I can attest to the value of strategic relationships. How important they are to the worldwide advancement of the Kingdom of God! Make no mistake about it. The devil also recognizes the value of these relationships, so he does everything in his power to destroy them.

Elisha and Naaman

There are a number of strategic relationships in God's Word. One of these relationships began to develop between an influential Syrian military leader and God's prophet Elisha. It could have produced a breakthrough for the nation of Israel.

The fifth chapter of the Book of 2 Kings tells of the high rank and special favor Naaman had with the king of Syria, for it was Naaman who led the armies of Syria to victory over the surrounding nations.

Upon close observation, we find that the Word of God makes an interesting statement about this heathen, military man. Naaman made his mighty conquests with the help of Jehovah God.

> **... because by him [Naaman] the Lord had
> given deliverance [victory] unto Syria....**
> **2 Kings 5:1**

While it does not state what God's interest in him was, it is evident God had plans for Naaman. However, He never fully realized His plans. The reason for this failure lies with Elisha's servant, Gehazi, for he had not learned that certain strategic relationships are infinitely more valuable than money.

The good news about Naaman is that God had blessed him. However, this description of Naaman doesn't end on a positive note, for the Bible goes on to tell us that Naaman was a leper.

> **... but he was a leper.**
> **2 Kings 5:1**

Verse two gives us more information about God's plan for bringing Naaman into a closer relationship with Himself.

> **... the Syrians had gone out by companies,
> and had brought away captive out of the land of
> Israel a little maid; and she waited on Naaman's
> wife.**
> **2 Kings 5:2**

Unknown to Naaman or his household, her captivity placed one of God's faithful servants inside the house of the captain of the hosts of Syria. Notice that she did her part, for she spoke up at exactly the right time. Hear the message of hope she brought to Naaman's house.

And she said unto her mistress, Would God my lord were with the prophet that is in Samaria! for he would recover him of his leprosy.
2 Kings 5:3

Just a few words from a little slave girl put world-changing events into motion. These events soon place the number-two man in all of Syria into a strategic relationship with God's prophet Elisha.

When Naaman arrives at the prophet's house, Elisha doesn't even come out to meet him. He simply sends his servant, Gehazi, out to speak to him. The servant brings the simplest of instructions to this great general. He tells Naaman to go to the River Jordan and dip seven times. When Naaman obeys, a wonderful miracle takes place, for God instantly heals him of the leprosy.

Then went he [Naaman] down, and dipped himself seven times in Jordan, according to the saying of the man of God: and his flesh came again like unto the flesh of a little child, and he was clean.
2 Kings 5:14

Notice the significance of what has happened. God has miraculously healed the captain of the army that holds the nation of Israel captive.

The next events that take place go beyond the expectation of the casual reader, for Naaman solemnly swears allegiance to Jehovah God.

> ... Behold, now I know that there is no God
> in all the earth, but in Israel. ...
> And Naaman said ... thy servant will
> henceforth offer neither burnt offering nor
> sacrifice unto other gods, but unto [Jehovah].
> **2 Kings 5:15,17**

The obvious conclusion is that Naaman is converted to the God of Israel.

Passing up the Big Offering

Upon returning to Elisha's house, Naaman makes a tremendous gesture of gratitude. He offers much treasure to the prophet for his deliverance. Immediately, the prophet realizes the priceless relationship God is setting up between himself and the man who holds the key to the release of Israel from bondage. Without hesitation, Elisha refuses the money Naaman wants to give him. Instead, he looks to the future and sees the potential blessing this prominent man can be to the Kingdom of God. In refusing the money, Elisha deepens the relationship that is rapidly developing between himself and Naaman.

> ... As the Lord liveth, before whom I stand,
> I will receive none. And he [Naaman] urged him
> to take it; but he [Elisha] refused.
> **2 Kings 5:16**

With this refusal, Elisha is saying that a favorable relationship with the most powerful man in the Syrian army is much more valuable than any benefit Naaman's money could bring.

Greed and Ignorance Destroy the Relationship

Now let's see how the greed and ignorance of Elisha's servant, Gehazi, bring an end to the strategic relationship God has established.

Running after Naaman under false pretenses, Gehazi takes from him two talents of silver and two garments. In a brief moment, this greedy servant ends the beautiful relationship God was forming between Elisha and the number-two man in Syria. Gehazi hinders the plan of God because he does not understand that certain key relationships are more valuable than money. Hear the prophet's words as he chastens his wicked servant.

> . . . Is it a time to receive money, and to receive garments, and oliveyards, and vineyards, and sheep, and oxen, and menservants, and maidservants?
> The leprosy therefore of Naaman shall cleave unto thee, and unto thy seed for ever. And he went out from his presence a leper as white as snow.
>
> 2 Kings 5:26,27

Sometimes it is better not to collect an offering but instead to develop an important relationship, one that will be much more valuable than the money of the offering could ever be.

Jesus Gets Thrown out of Town

There is another story of a strategic relationship in the Gospels. It took place when Jesus was enjoying immense popularity. Mark tells us He was regularly preaching in the synagogues throughout all Galilee. It is obvious that this freedom made the job of spreading the gospel much easier. This strategic relationship with the leaders of Galilee gave our Lord access to every pulpit in the region.

> **And he preached in their synagogues throughout all Galilee, and cast out devils.**
> **Mark 1:39**

Now notice as all this favor comes to an abrupt end. Verse 40 tells of a leper who comes to Jesus, asking Him to make him whole.

> **And there came a leper to him, beseeching him . . . saying unto him, If thou wilt, thou canst make me clean.**
> **Mark 1:40**

Jesus graciously heals the man.

> **And Jesus, moved with compassion, put forth his hand, and touched him, and saith unto him, I will; be thou clean.**
> **Mark 1:41**

Jesus Gives Specific Instructions

Now notice carefully as Jesus gives this man some specific instructions. If he obeys, the man's actions will strengthen our Lord's relationship with the leaders of Galilee. However, if he disobeys, he will bring to a close the strategic relationship Jesus is enjoying.

> **. . . See thou *say nothing to any man:* but go thy way, *show thyself to the priest,* and *offer for thy cleansing those things which Moses commanded,* for a testimony unto them.**
> **Mark 1:44**

The Bible tells us the man totally ignores our Lord's directions. Instead of showing himself to the priest, he takes to the street, broadcasting the miracle to the multitudes. *Neither does he make the required offering.* The events that followed are sad, to say the least, for by his disobedience, the man ends the relationship Jesus had enjoyed. He apparently did save the cost of the required offering, but at what a cost to Jesus' ministry!

> **Instead he went out and began to talk freely, spreading the news. As a result, Jesus could no longer enter a town openly but stayed outside in lonely places. . . .**
> **Mark 1:45, NIV**

The man's disobedience ruined the relationship between Jesus and the leaders of the Galilean synagogues. How important this relationship had been to our Lord! It was infinitely more valuable than the money the man saved by not making the prescribed offering.

A Personal Experience

A number of years ago, I was privileged to be involved with a preacher who had been a rather famous rock and roll star. He had also been quite successful as an entertainer in Las Vegas.

Shortly after I met him, a wealthy hotel and casino owner from Las Vegas was converted to Christ. God gloriously saved this hotel owner, and he immediately wanted to do everything he could to reach the people of Las Vegas with the gospel of Jesus Christ. He contacted the former rock and roll star and asked him to help present Christ to his city. They made plans for a giant gospel program featuring the best preachers and singers in the nation. It was going to be a week-long, annual event that would go on until Jesus comes.

Word Gets Out

Because of this extraordinary event, the hotel owner issued many press releases. He had set up a substantial advertising budget. He did everything first class and at full speed ahead. There can be no question about it. God was forming a key relationship with this Las Vegas multi-millionaire.

Then it happened. The information about the casino owner's conversion became known across the country. Well, as much as I hate to admit it, a feeding frenzy followed. A number of so-called ministers from across the nation descended upon the city. Every fund raiser who heard about this man's conversion passed through the hotel trying to get him to donate some money.

The Relationship Is Broken

Finally, my phone rang one night. It was my friend, the former rock and roll star. Tearfully, he told me of the abuses that were taking place. Ministers were asking for complimentary rooms, then leaving hundreds of dollars in unpaid telephone bills. Some left unpaid room-service bills that would make a spoiled aristocrat seem conservative. They left unpaid charges for limousine service, and even for clothes and jewelry from the exclusive shops in the lobby of the hotel. My friend told me the hotel owner finally closed his office door to Christians. He not only did that, but he also all but closed his pocketbook to paying for the remainder of the meeting.

How different all this would have been if the Gehazis of our day would have left this new convert alone. There would now be an annual Jesus festival on the strip in Las Vegas. God and the owner of one of the biggest casinos in our land would have a great relationship.

Instead, ignorant men moved in and snapped up some quick cash, leaving behind yet another ruined relationship.

When God Saves the Rich and Famous

How hard it is to convince the children of God that new converts who come to Christ from among the rich and famous, have something *much more valuable to bring to the Kingdom of God than their money.* They have influence in the world system. Oh, when will we learn that strategic relationships with these movers and shakers are infinitely more valuable than their money! If we would only stop and ask ourselves the question Elisha asked Gehazi, how many of these wonderful people would we spare?

> . . . Is it a time to receive money? . . .
> **2 Kings 5:26**

I think not, for strategic relationships are far more valuable than money!

9

The Reproach of Christ

**For we cannot but speak the things which
we have seen and heard.**
Acts 4:20

It is common knowledge that not all Christians feel the reproach of Christ. While no one wants to admit it, there is a way of living that avoids the persecution that comes with a bold Christian witness.

Many Secret Disciples

Even during Jesus' earthly life, it was common for people to avoid the reproach of Christ. The Bible tells of a prominent Jewish leader who respected and loved our Lord. However, rather than face reproach from the Jews, he chose not to identify publicly with Him.

**... Joseph of Arimathea, being a disciple of
Jesus, but secretly for fear of the Jews...**
John 19:38

Nicodemus, a ruler of the Jews, was an admirer of Jesus. However, even this well-known Bible character chose the cover of night to make his visit to our Lord.

**There was a man of the Pharisees, named
Nicodemus, a ruler of the Jews:**
The same came to Jesus by night. ...
John 3:1,2

The Torments of Fear

As we search the Scripture for a cause for these times of denial, the problem quickly becomes evident. *Fear* is the common denominator always present when there is hesitancy to identify publicly with our Lord.

The fear of identifying with an unpopular cause made the disciples withdraw from Jesus. Not only did they withdraw, but they openly denied knowing Him. Even the courageous boasting of Simon Peter couldn't stand up to the terror of that night. Hear him as he proclaims his undying loyalty.

> **Peter answered and said unto him, Though all men shall be offended because of thee, yet will I never be offended.**
> **Matthew 26:33**

These are magnificent words. However, our Lord knew how shallow they really were. Hear Him as He re-emphasizes His knowledge of total denial. He speaks directly to Simon and says, "Simon, you will not deny me once, but three times before the dawn."

> **Jesus said unto him, Verily I say unto thee, That this night, before the cock crow, thou shalt deny me thrice.**
> **Matthew 26:34**

We all know the outcome of this discussion, for all of His disciples denied Him and left Him before the awful events of that night were over. In every case fear caused the betrayal.

A Better Day

Let's not let these dark events in the lives of our Lord's disciples sound a negative tone. I am glad to report that since those days of denial, millions have boldly stood as His disciples. Not only have they stood, but millions of others have willingly died for their testimony of our Lord.

Secular history goes on to tell us that all but one of the disciples were put to death for their unflinching witness of Jesus. The one disciple who died of natural causes was John the Beloved. Now don't get the idea that John went through life without suffering reproach for Christ. In his lifetime he was beaten, boiled in oil, and banished to the Isle of Patmos for his bold testimony of the Lord Jesus.

More Valuable Than Treasures

Moses knew the reproach of Christ was more valuable than money. The Word of God makes a clear statement about him in the Book of Hebrews.

> **By faith Moses, when he was come to years, refused to be called the son of Pharaoh's daughter;**
> **Choosing rather to suffer affliction with the people of God, than to enjoy the pleasures of sin for a season;**
> ***Esteeming the reproach of Christ greater riches than the treasures in Egypt. . . .***
> **Hebrews 11:24-26**

Moses lived hundreds of years before the birth of our Lord. However, we have written proof that even before Jesus' birth, the reproach of Christ was more valuable than many treasures. Please realize that during the lifetime of

Moses, Egypt was the leading nation on earth. It was wealthy beyond measure. However, Moses quickly concluded that the reproach of Christ would be more valuable than all the money in Egypt. How could he make such a decision?

Notice that Moses saw something. By faith, he saw that a large reward comes to those who suffer reproach for our Lord.

> **... for he had respect unto the recompense of the reward.**
> **Hebrews 11:26**

Moses was sure God would reward him, and you can be sure God will reward you.

> **Blessed are they which are persecuted for righteousness' sake: for theirs is the kingdom of heaven.**
> **Blessed are ye, when men shall revile you, and persecute you, and shall say all manner of evil against you falsely, for my sake.**
> **Rejoice, and be exceeding glad: for great is your reward in heaven: for so persecuted they the prophets which were before you.**
> **Matthew 5:10-12**

Reproach Over Compromise

The Apostle Paul came to the same conclusion Moses did. He faced the choice of identifying with the world system or with our Lord. Paul could have chosen not to suffer the reproach of Christ. He could have been a secret saint. Like Nicodemus, he could have come to Jesus only at night. However, he determined that momentarily suffering reproach for Christ was infinitely more valuable than the momentary enjoyment of pleasures in this world.

> **For I reckon that the sufferings of this present time are not worthy to be compared with the glory which shall be revealed in us.**
> **Romans 8:18**

Paul decided the price he would pay for standing for Christ was well worth it in order to gain the glory Christ brings.

The Grave Is Not Final

Three glorious things belong to those who suffer reproach for Christ. First, they become part of a select company of men and women who know beyond any shadow of a doubt that the grave is not final. They are witnesses to the resurrection of Christ, knowing God will resurrect them to live eternally with the Lord. Let us once again hear the Apostle Paul as he speaks to Timothy.

> **Be not thou therefore ashamed of the testimony of our Lord, nor of me his prisoner: but be thou partaker of the afflictions of the gospel according to the power of God;**
> **Who hath saved us, and called us with an holy calling. . . .**
> **For the which cause I also suffer these things: nevertheless I am not ashamed: for I know whom I have believed, and am persuaded that he is able to keep that which I have committed unto him against that day.**
> **2 Timothy 1:8,9,12**

God's Power Becomes Your Power

The second glorious thing is that those who suffer the reproach of Christ receive from the Holy Ghost the power to stand for Him.

> **But ye shall receive power, after that the Holy Ghost is come upon you: and ye shall be witnesses unto me both in Jerusalem, and in all Judea, and in Samaria, and unto the uttermost part of the earth.**
>
> Acts 1:8

Nowhere was this power to witness in the face of opposition more evident than in the life of the well-known Christian martyr, Stephen.

> **. . . they chose Stephen, a man full of faith and of the Holy Ghost. . . .**
> **. . . Stephen, full of faith and power. . .**
>
> Acts 6:5,8

It is interesting that the word *power* in these verses is the Greek word *dunamis,* from which comes our word *dynamite.*

> **But ye shall receive *power,* after that the Holy Ghost is come upon you: and ye shall be witnesses unto me. . . .**
>
> Acts 1:8

The Holy Ghost gives the believer extraordinary ability and power to be an unflinching witness. Stephen became this type of witness. His words convicted his enemies so much that they stoned him to death.

Notice the link between Stephen and Moses. They both chose to suffer reproach rather than deny the Lord. Their decisions were not just religious zeal, for they both saw something. They saw Him who is invisible.

> **By faith [Moses] forsook Egypt, not fearing the wrath of the king: for he endured, as seeing him who is invisible.**
>
> **Hebrews 11:27**

Now hear the same words about Stephen.

> **But [Stephen], being full of the Holy Ghost, looked up steadfastly into heaven, and saw the glory of God, and Jesus standing on the right hand of God.**
>
> **And said, Behold, I see the heavens opened, and the Son of man standing on the right hand of God.**
>
> **Acts 7:55**

Those whom Jesus has truly filled with the power of the Holy Ghost, are able to bear the reproach of Christ.

A Lasting Reward

The third benefit of bearing reproach for Christ is the unfading reward God promises.

> **Blessed be the God and Father of our Lord Jesus Christ, which according to his abundant mercy hath begotten us again unto a lively hope by the resurrection of Jesus Christ from the dead,**
>
> **To an inheritance incorruptible, and undefiled, and *that fadeth not away*, reserved in heaven for you.**
>
> **1 Peter 1:3,4**

The Apostle Paul describes the reward this way.

> **I have fought a good fight, I have finished my course, I have kept the faith:**
>
> **Henceforth there is laid up for me a crown of righteousness, which the Lord, the righteous judge, shall give me at that day: and not to me only, but unto all them also that love his appearing.**
>
> **2 Timothy 4:7,8**

True Holiness Brings Persecution

Persecution is unavoidable to those who live godly lives. Paul makes this truth clear in his letter to young Timothy.

> **. . . all that will live godly in Christ Jesus shall suffer persecution.**
>
> **2 Timothy 3:12**

Denying our Lord brings eternal loss.

> **Whosoever therefore shall confess me before men, him will I confess also before my Father which is in heaven.**
>
> **But whosoever shall deny me before men, him will I also deny before my Father which is in heaven.**
>
> **Matthew 10:32,33**

Add to these scriptures the words Paul spoke to Timothy, and the choice is simple.

> **If we suffer, we shall also reign with him: if we deny him, he also will deny us.**
>
> **2 Timothy 2:12**

Those whom God has redeemed can make only one choice. If you know that you know that He is risen, *denying Him is out of the question.*

> **For we cannot but speak the things which
> we have seen and heard.**
> **Acts 4:20**

The reproach of Christ is more valuable than any worldly treasure.

10

Worshiping the True and Living God

...so panteth my soul after thee, O God.
Psalm 42:1

When studying the life of our Lord Jesus Christ, it becomes evident that the worship of the true and living God is more valuable than all of the wealth, power, and prestige of the whole world. Jesus is the pattern Son. He is the one who has gone before us to show us the way. It's no surprise then, that He first brings this truth to light. If you remember, our Lord flatly turned down the devil's offer to give up worshiping the true and living God and start worshiping him. I am sure the devil thought he had made the deal so sweet that Jesus would not be able to refuse.

Jesus Tested

The account I am speaking of took place immediately after our Lord's baptism. It was at this time that God the Father openly declared the divine relationship that existed between Himself and His Son Jesus.

> And Jesus, when he was baptized, went up straightway out of the water: and, lo, the heavens were opened unto him, and he saw the Spirit of God descending like a dove, and lighting upon him:

**And lo a voice from heaven, saying, This is
my beloved Son, in whom I am well pleased.
Matthew 3:16,17**

As soon as God makes this announcement, the Spirit
leads Jesus into the wilderness to be tempted (tested) by
the evil one (Matthew 4:1).

When the testing begins, it comes in the form of three
powerful temptations. First the devil asks Jesus to prove
He is the Son of God by turning stones into bread. This
idea is especially tempting to our Lord, because He has
just finished forty days of fasting and is extremely hungry.
The devil focuses the second temptation on our Lord's
ego, for he suggests that He jump from the pinnacle of the
temple and emerge from the bottom of the gorge without
injury. Imagine how impressive this feat would be to
everyone.

In the third test, the devil tries to turn the heart of our
Lord from the Father by offering Him the wealth of the
world.

All of this world's goods would be His if He would
only bow the knee to Satan. In answering the devil's offer,
our Lord clearly shows that worshiping the true and living
God is more valuable than all the wealth the world
contains.

**Again, the devil taketh him up into an
exceeding high mountain, and showeth him all
the kingdoms of the world, and the glory of them;
And saith unto him, All these things will I
give thee, if thou wilt fall down and worship me.**

Then saith Jesus unto him, Get thee hence, Satan: for it is written, Thou shalt worship the Lord thy God, and him only shalt thou serve.
Matthew 4:8-10

Notice how much more value Jesus places on the worship of Jehovah God than anything the world has to offer. Jesus didn't hesitate, for He knew the wonderful privilege of worshiping God Jehovah was more valuable than money!

The Psalmist Testifies

The psalmist is also clear about the value of worshiping the true and living God. He says one day in God's house is worth more than three years of doing anything else. He also states that just being the doorkeeper at God's house would be more valuable than holding a position of honor among the wicked of the world.

For a day in thy courts is better than a thousand. I had rather be a doorkeeper in the house of my God, than to dwell in the tents of wickedness.
Psalm 84:10

Notice the next verses. They tell us the psalmist doesn't believe his rejection of the world system and choosing worship in God's house will cost him the good things of life.

For the Lord God is a sun and shield: the Lord will give grace and glory: *no good thing will he withhold from them that walk uprightly.*

O Lord of hosts, blessed is the man that trusteth in thee.
Psalm 84:11,12

Notice the benefits he lists that go along with worshiping God. He says God is light (sun) and protection (shield), and a giver of unmerited favor (grace). He will not withhold one good thing from the upright. He blesses the man who walks uprightly.

Daniel's Time With God

It would not be right to speak of the value of worshiping Jehovah God without telling of Daniel and the great value he placed on his daily prayer and worship time with the God of heaven. The story begins in the sixth chapter of the Book of Daniel. Here we see that Daniel has come into special favor with King Darius.

This chapter tells us that King Darius sets 120 princes over the business of his kingdom. Then he chooses Daniel to be their chief overseer. Daniel's prestige is so great that the princes become jealous of him and plan an evil scheme to have him put to death. They trick the king by encouraging him to make a vain decree. They get him to pass a law that makes it illegal to pray to anyone except the king for thirty days. The decree simply says that if any person in the kingdom dares to pray to anyone except King Darius, he will be thrown into a den of hungry lions that will tear him apart.

The enemies of Daniel are aware that he prays three times each day to the God of heaven. Now the question is, Just how valuable is Daniel's time of worship to him? Think about it. He would have to give it up for only thirty days. Well, I am sure you know the answer. However, let's see it again from God's Word.

> Now when Daniel knew that the writing was signed, he went into his house; and his windows being open in his chamber toward Jerusalem, he kneeled upon his knees three times a day, and prayed, and gave thanks before his God....
> Then these men ... found Daniel praying....
> Then ... they ... said before the king, That Daniel ... regardeth not ... the decree that thou hast signed, but maketh his petition three times a day.
> Then the king commanded, and they brought Daniel, and cast him into the den of lions....
>
> **Daniel 6:10,11,13,16**

Daniel's decision makes it clear that worshiping Jehovah God is more valuable to him than even life itself. He boldly continued to pray as always. Why, he even had the windows open so that everyone could see him.

To make a long story short, Daniel survived the night in the lion's den and emerged the next morning without even a scratch. Oh, lest I forget to mention it, being a fair man, the king then gave Daniel's enemies their turn in the lion's den. Yes, you guessed it. The lions tore them to pieces.

> And the king commanded, and they brought those men which had accused Daniel, and they cast them into the den of lions ... and the lions had the mastery of them, and brake all their bones in pieces or ever they came at the bottom of the den.
>
> **Daniel 6:24**

History is filled with the accounts of brave men and women who have given their treasures and riches and even their very lives, instead of giving up the privilege of worshiping the great God Jehovah. It is no contest. Worshiping the true and living God is worth more than money or even life itself.

11

Your Eternal Soul

... we have ... an anchor of the soul. ...
Hebrews 6:19

Scripture tells us God formed man from the dust of the earth. Then He breathed the breath of His Spirit into the man he had formed. When the breath of God merged with his flesh, the man became a living soul.

> **And the Lord God formed man of the dust of the ground, and breathed into his nostrils the breath of life; and man became a living soul.**
> **Genesis 2:7**

The Soul's Value

Scripture tells us the soul remains in a conscious state throughout eternity. This eternally conscious part of man is more valuable than all the wealth the world possesses. Let's hear this truth from the Lord Jesus Christ Himself.

> **For what is a man profited, if he shall gain the whole world, and lose his own soul? or what shall a man give in exchange for his soul?**
> **Matthew 16:26**

Jesus makes it plain and simple. The man who loses his soul has lost everything. He has suffered loss beyond measure, for you cannot place a price on an eternal soul. There still isn't enough money in the world to equal its value.

When I try to explain the eternal value of a soul, one of our Lord's parables always comes to mind. It is the story of the rich farmer who totally misjudged the infinite value of his eternal soul. If you remember, he tore down his barns and built larger ones. He then foolishly ordered his soul to be content with the things he had bought with his money. Hear him as he reasons with himself and plans for his soul's comfort.

> **And I will say to my soul, Soul, thou hast much goods laid up for many years; take thine ease, eat, drink, and be merry.**
> **Luke 12:19**

Everything seems to be going well until God abruptly speaks, declaring the man to be a fool. Not only that, but God reveals He will require his soul that very night. Worst of all, the man is not ready to meet God, for his soul is unregenerate, and he is not prepared for eternity.

> **But God said unto him, Thou fool, this night thy soul shall be required of thee. . . .**
> **Luke 12:20**

No Fool Like a Rich Fool

Jesus gives another example of a man who misjudged the value of his eternal soul and ended up in hell. Luke tells the story about a beggar named Lazarus and a rich man. The rich man lived a prosperous life. To put it plainly, he had everything.

> **There was a certain rich man, which was clothed in purple and fine linen, and fared sumptuously every day.**
> **Luke 16:19**

There is a fatal flaw in this rich man's thinking process, for he is selfish and unsympathetic. He regularly passes by the beggar without even caring.

> **And there was a certain beggar named Lazarus, which was laid at his gate, full of sores,**
> **And desiring to be fed with the crumbs which fell from the rich man's table. . . .**
> **Luke 16:20,21**

Now the story takes on a new twist. The rich man dies, but much to his surprise, he is still conscious. His eyes work. He is able to feel pain. He is thirsty. He has memories, for he now begins to care about his lost loved ones back home.

> **And in hell he lift up his eyes, being in torments, and seeth Abraham afar off, and Lazarus in his bosom.**
> **And he cried and said, Father Abraham, have mercy on me, and send Lazarus, that he may dip the tip of his finger in water, and cool my tongue; for I am tormented in this flame.**
> **But Abraham said, Son, remember that thou in thy lifetime receivedst thy good things, and likewise Lazarus evil things: but now he is comforted, and thou art tormented. . . .**
> **Then he said, I pray thee therefore, father, that thou wouldest send him to my father's house:**
> **For I have five brethren; that he may testify unto them, lest they also come into this place of torment.**
> **Luke 16:23-25,27,28**

Think about it. This man lived his whole life without making any provision for his soul. Then, rich as he was before his death, he was not primarily thinking of his money. His main thoughts were of the precious souls of his five lost brothers who were still alive. It is as our Lord said.

> **For what is a man profited, if he shall gain**
> **the whole world, and lose his own soul? or what**
> **shall a man give in exchange for his soul?**
> **Matthew 16:26**

There is no comparison between the pleasure and power of wealth during your short lifetime, and an eternity in hell. If you gain the whole world and have to give your soul to get it, you have made the poorest of bargains. Even the worst sinner would have to admit that an eternal soul is more valuable than all the wealth this world can produce.

Eternal Torment

The last verse in the wonderful Book of Isaiah tells of the eternal state of those who misjudge the value of their eternal souls.

> **. . . go forth, and look upon the carcasses of**
> **the men that have transgressed against me: for**
> **their worm shall not die, neither shall their fire**
> **be quenched. . . .**
> **Isaiah 66:24**

> **. . . what shall a man give in exchange for**
> **his soul?**
> **Matthew 16:26**

12

The Precious Blood of Jesus

. . . the precious blood. . .
1 Peter 1:19

There is a fountain filled with blood
Drawn from Immanuel's veins;
And sinners, plunged beneath that flood,
Lose all their guilty stains.*

Oh! precious is the flow
That makes me white as snow;
No other fount I know,
Nothing but the blood of Jesus.**

When it comes to the blood, apostles have filled the
Holy Writ, poets have written volumes, songwriters have
harmonized, and preachers have sermonized. However, it
still remains the wonder of wonders. I speak of nothing
less than the precious blood of Jesus, that crimson flow
that means so much to so many people. Why, the mere
mention of that precious flow never fails to stir the hearts
of those who have benefitted from its cleansing effect.

---

*   *Words by William Cowper, 1731-1800*
**   *Words by Robert Lowry, 1826-1899*

The blood of Jesus moves all of Christianity as nothing else can. It is the most precious thing the Church possesses.

A Big Subject

There probably is no subject in Christianity we can say more about than the precious blood of our Lord and Savior Jesus Christ. Several theologians in our century have written entire books on this topic. Because of the vastness of its scope, it becomes extremely difficult to write about it in just one chapter. Therefore, this chapter will just barely scratch the surface. I will write only a few words about the blood in these four areas: its power to divide, unite, and save, and its pricelessness.

The Blood Divides

In the sixth chapter of John, an event illustrates the tremendous power the blood possesses to divide. It is a season when our Lord's popularity is probably at its peak. Many people have come to hear Him teach. At this point of His ministry Jesus begins to reveal the deeper truth about Himself as the bread of life. If you notice, He states this great truth in a very matter-of-fact way.

> . . . my Father giveth you the true bread from heaven.
>
> For the bread of God is he which cometh down from heaven, and giveth life unto the world.
>
> John 6:32,33

Hear the people as they encourage Him to tell them more about this bread that comes from heaven.

> . . . Lord, evermore give us this bread.
> John 6:34

Notice how Jesus takes this teaching to depths that eventually cause division.

> . . . Jesus said unto them, I am the bread of life. . . .
> John 6:35

This teaching goes on until verse 53. Here Jesus speaks the words that abruptly bring separation.

> . . . Verily, verily, I say unto you, Except ye *eat the flesh* of the Son of man, and *drink his blood*, ye have no life in you.
> John 6:53

We see the culmination of this division in verse 66 where the writer tells us,

> From that time many of his disciples went back, and walked no more with him.
> John 6:66

This result is typical of the blood of our Lord, for it has always been a point of division.

I would like to share an event that took place many years ago when I was pastoring in Denver, Colorado. For some reason, I was in a meeting with a prominent member from the largest liberal church in the city. The reason for the meeting escapes me at this time. However, I will never forget something he said to me.

As soon as he realized I was a pastor, he began to tell me of the wonderful project his church had just completed. He said they had successfully edited out of their old church hymnal, every song that had any mention of the blood in it. When I heard these words, I immediately asked why in the world anyone would want to do such a horrible thing. His reply almost floored me. He said, "We want to rid ourselves of the stigma of the slaughterhouse religion."

That was all I could take. My next words strongly reaffirmed my love and loyalty for the blood of our Lord, and its absolute necessity for salvation. Needless to say, that was the last I ever heard from that misguided church member.

The Blood Unites

Strange as it may seem, the same blood that so powerfully separates, also unites. Notice the special word the Apostle Paul uses when he describes the Lord's Supper.

> I speak as to wise men; judge ye what I say.
> The cup of blessing which we bless, is it not
> the communion of the blood of Christ? . . .
> 1 Corinthians 10:15,16

In the King James Version, the word translated *communion* is somewhat vague. It comes from the Greek word *koinonia*. Strong's concordance gives it a more potent definition. It comes from a root word meaning "*partnership,* namely, participation or social intercourse." It literally means "to communicate, communion, distribution, fellowship." *Koinonia* is talking about joining together in close relationship. As you can see, the very blood that caused many of His disciples to walk with Him no longer (John 6), is the very element that draws all the members of the body of Christ together. The eating of our Lord's flesh and the drinking of His blood in the ordinance of Holy Communion is probably the part of Christianity in which the Church participates with the most union. In this ordinance, the Church and the blood of our Lord come together in fellowship from one end of the earth to the other. The blood is powerful in its ability to unite believers.

The Blood Saves

The salvation of a lost soul is still, without a doubt, the most important miracle God ever performs. To take a lost, hell-bound sinner and turn him into a heaven-bound son or daughter of God is a wonder without parallel. It involves God's taking a sinner, one He cannot even look upon, and redeeming him. The word *redeem* means to "ransom or buy something back." The blood of Jesus paid the price to ransom us.

> **Forasmuch as ye know that ye were not redeemed with corruptible things, as silver and gold, from your vain conversation received by tradition from your fathers;**
> **But with the precious blood of Christ. . . .**
> **1 Peter 1:18,19**

If a person's plan of salvation does not involve the blood, the Bible says it will not stand.

> **. . . almost all things are by the law purged with blood; and without shedding of blood is no remission.**
> **Hebrews 9:22**

My own circumstances continue to bring me into a deeper and deeper revelation of the vast worth of the blood. It is precious blood, for it saves.

When I accepted Christ, I confessed and forsook tremendous sins. I have testified of the transformation and the absolute change of everything in my life. However, God also forgave me of things no one but Jesus and I know about, things I could not have forgotten. When He saw the blood that Jesus shed for me, the Father instantly forgave those sins and cast them into His sea of forgetfulness, never to remember them against me again.

The Blood Is Priceless

The Apostle Peter plainly says the blood of Jesus is priceless.

> **Forasmuch as ye know that ye were not redeemed with corruptible things, as *silver and gold*, from your vain conversation received by tradition from your fathers;**
> **But with the precious blood of Christ, as of a lamb without blemish and without spot.**
> **1 Peter 1:18,19**

I could say much more; however, I leave this chapter simply saying that the blood of Jesus is much more valuable than gold or silver. It is, without a doubt, the most valuable thing in the universe.

13

The Anointing

> . . . he didn't realize that the Lord had left him.
>
> **Judges 16:20**

The fact that the anointing is more valuable than money is evident to all those who have ever felt its power come upon their lives.

There is a place in Scripture where the Lord shows us the infinite superiority and value of the anointing over mere money. It becomes evident in the life of an opportunist named Simon the Sorcerer. He is present when one of the first gospel campaigns takes place. Simon sees the great power of the Word of God, and as he observes the preaching of the gospel, he gives lip service and verbally accepts Christ.

> **Then Simon himself believed also. . . .**
> **Acts 8:13**

If only Simon had allowed this encounter to truly cleanse his heart, how differently his story would have ended. However, as he observed the phenomenon that accompanies the filling of the Holy Ghost, he was stirred to monetary gain instead of to spiritual progress. Hear him as he tries to buy the anointing that brings about the filling of the Holy Ghost.

> . . . when Simon saw that through laying on
> of the apostles' hands the Holy Ghost was given,
> he offered them money,
> Saying, Give me also this power, that on
> whomsoever I lay hands, he may receive the Holy
> Ghost.
> **Acts 8:18,19**

What a flawed judgment this man had! Instead of eagerly grabbing the money, Simon Peter rebuked him and told him of the evil that had come into his heart.

> But Peter said unto him, Thy money perish
> with thee, because thou hast thought that the gift
> of God may be purchased with money.
> Thou hast neither part nor lot in this
> matter: for thy heart is not right in the sight of
> God.
> For I perceive that thou art in the gall of
> bitterness, and in the bond of iniquity.
> **Acts 8:20-23**

Samson's Anointing

Nowhere in Scripture is the anointing of God more visible than in the life of Samson. God had made him an anointed vessel from his mother's womb. However, Samson did not appreciate his anointing. The Word of God tells us he continually chose the pleasures of sin over the virtues of the godly life. He chose the ungodly Philistine women over the godly women of Israel. He was often in the company of harlots. He gambled and made sport with the offscouring of the earth. Finally we see him languishing in the lap of Delilah, telling her the secret things of God.

Eventually the day comes when God withdraws the precious anointing from him. Hear the biblical account.

> **And [Delilah] made [Samson] sleep upon her knees; and she called for a man, and she caused him to shave off the seven locks of his head; and she began to afflict him, and his strength went from him.**
>
> **And she said, The Philistines be upon thee, Samson. And he awoke out of his sleep, and said, I will go out as at other times before, and shake myself. And he wist not that the Lord was departed from him.**
>
> **But the Philistines took him, and put out his eyes, and brought him down to Gaza, and bound him with fetters of brass; and he did grind in the prison house.**
>
> **Judges 16:19-21**

Here we see a most pitiful event. God removes the anointing from His appointed servant. The Philistines blind Samson and bind him like an ox. Instead of being the champion of God, he becomes the chump of Satan. Now he grinds at the mill for the heathen.

Sometimes losing the anointing is the only thing that will open the eyes of men and women who lose track of its value. Hear Samson as he pleads to feel the power of God in his bones just one more time. He is now ready to pay with his life if the anointing will only return and let him once again taste the victory of God.

> **And Samson called unto the Lord, and said, O Lord God, remember me, I pray thee, and strengthen me, I pray thee, only this once, O**

God, that I may be at once avenged of the Philistines for my two eyes.

And Samson took hold of the two middle pillars upon which the house stood, and on which it was borne up, of the one with his right hand, and of the other with his left.

And Samson said, Let me die with the Philistines. And he bowed himself with all his might; and the house fell upon the lords, and upon all the people that were therein. So the dead which he slew at his death were more than they which he slew in his life.

Judges 16:28-30

Thank God for His forgiveness and His grace in reinstating the anointing of Samson. However, we cannot help but wonder how much greater the ending of this story would have been, if Samson would have valued his anointing in the beginning of his life as much as he did in the end.

A Big Mistake

Now let's look at the story of the misguided son of Isaac named Esau. His story is in the Book of Genesis.

Esau was the oldest son of Isaac. The birthright, or priesthood of the family, would one day be his.

. . . Esau was a cunning hunter, a man of the field; and Jacob was a plain man, dwelling in tents.

And Isaac loved Esau: . . . but Rebekah loved Jacob.

And Jacob sod pottage: and Esau came from the field, and he was faint:

> And Esau said to Jacob, Feed me . . . for I am faint. . . .
>
> And Jacob said, Sell me this day thy birthright.
>
> And Esau said, Behold, I am at the point to die: and what profit shall this birthright do to me?
>
> **Genesis 25:27-32**

There you have it. Esau had the anointing of God. It made him the spiritual leader of his brethren, but he sold it for a mere bowl of beans. It is not until you read the Book of Hebrews that you see how much Esau regretted the loss of his anointing.

> Lest there be any fornicator, or profane person, as Esau, who for one morsel of meat sold his birthright.
>
> For ye know how that afterward, when he would have inherited the blessing, he was rejected: for he found no place of repentance, though he sought it carefully *with tears*.
>
> **Hebrews 12:16,17**

My Anointing

In my own life there are treasures that are not for sale, nor will they ever be for sale. Among these is that precious power of God that came upon me, the day God called me to preach His precious Word. This great power took me from the bottom rung of life and has carried me throughout the earth. It has brought me into the presence of the greatest men of my day.

Please note that I do not measure these men as great by the yardstick of the world. I speak of the great men of God I have the privilege of knowing, some here and some now in heaven. This anointing has given to me, a near dropout from high school, the privilege of having written seventeen books that have all been best-sellers. It has allowed me to speak messages that have brought hundreds of millions of dollars into the hands of godly men and women. The anointing brings me by television three times each day into the homes of millions of believers in America as well as across the earth.

The next statement I make with all sincerity. If I were offered a billion dollars for my anointing, if the cash were on the table and someone had already paid the taxes, without hesitation, I would say no. You might say, "Why, Brother John, that's a mighty big statement. Are you sure?" Yes, I know I am speaking the truth, for I once had to spend three years without the anointing. My foolishness cost me my ministry. During that time, the business world treated me better financially than anyone would believe. However, when the Holy Ghost of God called me and offered me the right to go back into the ministry, I left the business world that same morning. I left in spite of the fact that if I had stayed only sixty more days, I would have received my bonus for the whole year. That bonus would have been enough money to pay the salary I made during the first five years of my return to the ministry. It was an easy choice to make, especially after three years of absence from my precious anointing. Patricia and I forfeited a bonus equal to our wages for five years, rather than wait just sixty more days to return to the anointing.

With this said, I hope you have seen at least a glimpse of the value of the anointing of God. It is definitely worth more than money.

14

A Final Word

Now that you know these things that are better than money, my prayer is that this knowledge will help you achieve the balance you need to be all God wants you to be. However, I must also bring a final thought. It comes from the Word of God.

. . . money answereth all things.
Ecclesiastes 10:19

When he makes the statement that money answers all things, Solomon deals with the practical part of this book, for without money I could never have it published. Granted, many things are better than money. However, *everything worth having is dependent upon money.*

Think about it. Your good name, a good spouse, and the good Word of God are all dependent upon money. Even the message about the precious blood of Jesus, as valuable as it is, depends upon money. It takes money to carry the gospel from generation to generation and country to country.

Remember, Jesus had a treasurer who kept a bag of money for His ministry. The Apostle Paul says the plan of salvation depends on money and the faithful saint who gives it.

For whosoever shall call upon the name of the Lord shall be saved.

. . . how shall they hear without a preacher?

And how shall they preach, except they be sent? . . .

Romans 10:13-15

Yes, the gospel of salvation is free to those who receive it. However, it costs a tremendous amount of money to those who take the responsibility of sending it to others.

A Balanced View

No matter what your view of biblical economics might be, you now know there are things more desirable than money. As always, the entire Church stands ready to teach these great truths, for the answer to every problem lies in getting God's Word to a lost and dying world. There is only one thing missing. It is the money to send the message. This is why I teach biblical economics. This is why I have so much to say about money.

10% Discount

To order other books by John Avanzini and receive a 10 percent discount, complete both sides of this form and return it with your payment to HIS Publishing Co.

Qty	Title	Cost	Total
	Always Abounding	5.95	
	The Debt-Free Guarantee	5.95	
	The Debt Term-O-Nator	5.95	
	Faith Extenders	7.95	
	Financial Excellence	9.95	
	Hundredfold	7.95	
	It's Not Working, Brother John!	8.95	
	John Avanzini Answers Questions	6.95	
	Powerful Principles of Increase	8.95	
	Stolen Property Returned	5.95	
	The Wealth of the World	6.95	
	Things BetterThan Money	5.95	
	War on Debt	7.95	
	Rapid Debt-Reduction Strategies	12.95	
	The Victory Book	14.95	
	Have a Good Report	8.95	
	Subtotal		
	Less 10% Discount		
	Shipping & Handling		2.00
	Total Enclosed		

(   ) Enclosed is my check or money order made
        payable to **HIS Publishing Company**

Please charge my: (   ) Visa   (   ) MasterCard

(   ) Discover   (   ) American Express

Account # ☐☐☐☐☐☐☐☐☐☐☐☐☐☐☐☐

Expiration Date _____/_____/_____

Signature_____

To assure prompt and accurate delivery of your order,
please take the time to print all information neatly.

Name_____

Address_____

City_____State_____Zip_____

Area Code & Phone (_____)_____

Send mail orders to:

HIS Publishing Company

P.O. Box 917001

Ft. Worth, TX 76117-9001

TRINITY BROADCASTING NETWORK

An All-Christian Television Network Broadcasting the
Gospel 24 Hours a Day via Satellite, Cable TV and
Local TV Broadcast Stations

Alphabetical Directory of TBN Owned and Affiliate Station
(• Indicates an Affiliate-owned Station)

ALASKA
•Anchorage Ch. 22
•NORTH POLE Ch. 4
ALABAMA
•Berry Ch. 63
•Birmingham Ch. 51
•Decatur Ch. 22
Dothan Ch. 41
•Florence Ch. 57
•GADSDEN Ch. 60
Huntsville Ch. 64
•Huntsville Ch. 67
•MOBILE Ch. 21
•MONTGOMERY Ch. 45
•Opelika Ch. 35
Scottsboro/
Selma Ch. 52
Tuscaloosa Ch. 46
ARKANSAS
•DeQueen Ch. 8
Fayetteville Ch. 42
Ft. Smith Ch. 27
•Harrison Ch. 66
•Little Rock Ch. 33
Mountain Home Ch. 43
ARIZONA
Bullhead City Ch. 20
Cottonwood Ch. 58
•Duncan Ch 17
Flagstaff Ch. 62
Globe Ch. 63
•Lake Havasu Ch. 25
PHOENIX Ch. 21
•Safford Ch. 17
Shonto/Tonalea Ch. 38
•Sierra Vista Ch. 33
Tuscon Ch. 57
Tuscon Ch. 56
CALIFORNIA
Alturas Ch. 30
Atwater/Merced Ch. 57
Bakersfield Ch. 55
Desert Hot Sprgs. Ch. 40
•Fresno Ch. 56
•FRESNO Ch. 53
Lancaster/
Palmdale Ch. 54
•Lompoc Ch. 23

Monterey Ch. 53
Palm Springs Ch. 66
Porterville/
Visalia Ch. 15
Redding Ch. 65
Sacramento Ch. 69
•SAN JOSE Ch. 65
•San Luis Obispo Ch. 36
SANTA ANA Ch. 40
Santa Barbara Ch. 15
•Santa Maria Ch. 65
Ventura Ch. 45
Victorville Ch. 33
COLORADO
•Boulder Ch. 17
•Colorado Sprgs. Ch. 43
Denver Ch. 57
Denver Ch. 47
Denver Ch. 33
•Las Animas Ch.40
Loveland Ch. 48
•Pueblo Ch. 48
DELAWARE
Dover Ch. 67
•Wilmington Ch. 26
FLORIDA
•Alachua Ch. 69
Ft. Meyers Ch. 67
•FT. PIERCE Ch. 21
•JACKSONVILLE Ch. 59
Lake City Ch. 23
•LEESBURG/
ORLANDO Ch. 55
•Melbourne Ch. 62
MIAMI Ch. 45
•Sarasota Ch. 24
Sebring Ch 17
St. Petersburg 60
St. Petersburg Ch. 69
•Tallahassee Ch. 17
Tampa Ch. 68
•W. Palm Beach Ch. 47
GEORGIA
Albany Ch. 23
ATLANTA Ch. 63
Augusta Ch. 65
Brunswick Ch. 33
•DALTON Ch. 23

•Hazelhurst Ch. 63
Marietta Ch. 55
Munroe Ch. 65
Savannah Ch. 67
Waycross Ch. 46
HAWAII
•HONOLULU Ch. 26
•KONA Ch. 6
IDAHO
Boise Ch. 47
Pocatello 15
Twin Falls Ch. 25
ILLINOIS
•Bloomington Ch. 64
Champaign/
Urbana Ch. 34
Decatur Ch. 29
•LaSALLE Ch. 35
•Marian Ch. 27
Palatine Ch. 36
•Peoria Ch. 41
•QUINCY Ch. 16
•Robinson Ch. 57
•Rockford Ch. 52
•Sterling Ch. 52
Waukegan Ch. 22
INDIANA
•ANGOLA/
FT. WAYNE Ch 63
BLOOMINGTON Ch. 42
CLARKSVILLE Ch. 26
Evansville Ch. 38
•Ft. Wayne Ch. 66
•Jeffersonville Ch. 5
Lafayette Ch. 36
Muncie Ch 32
Michigan City Ch. 24
RICHMOND Ch. 43
Terre Haute Ch. 65
IOWA
•Ames Ch. 52
Cedar Rapids Ch. 61
Davenport/
Bettendorf Ch. 58
•Des Moines Ch. 35
•Iowa City Ch. 64
•Keokuk Ch. 60
Ottumwa Ch. 42

Souix City Ch. 38
Waterloo Ch. 65
KANSAS
Junction City Ch. 25
Manhattan Ch. 31
Salina Ch. 15
Topeka Ch. 21
Wichita Ch. 59
KENTUCKY
•Beattyville Ch. 65
Corbin Ch. 41
Hopkinsville Ch. 62
•Paducah Ch. 54
LOUISIANA
Alexandria Ch. 19
Baton Rouge Ch. 56
•Lake Charles Ch. 51
Mermentau Ch. 45
Monroe Ch. 27
New Orleans Ch. 59
Shreveport Ch. 65
MASSACHUSETTS
Pittsfield Ch. 42
Springfield Ch. 67
MARYLAND
Cresaptown/
Cumberland Ch. 16
MAINE
•Bangor Ch. 17
•DANFORTH Ch. 17
•Farmington Ch. 21
•Machias Ch. 21
•Medway Ch. 14
•Portland Ch. 18
Presque Isle Ch. 51
MICHIGAN
Detroit Ch. 66
•JACKSON Ch. 59
•Kalamazoo Ch. 24
•Lancing Ch. 69
Muskegon Ch. 29
•MUSKEGON Ch. 54
•SAGINAW Ch. 49
Sault Ste Marie Ch. 67
MINNESOTA
Duluth Ch. 58
•Fairmont Ch. 28
Minneapolis Ch. 58
•New Ulm Ch. 22
Rochester Ch. 60
St. Cloud Ch. 19
•Wilmar Ch. 27
MISSOURI
•Branson Ch. 25
 Columbia Ch. 56
•Jefferson City Ch. 41
•Joplin Ch. 9
•Joplin/Carthage Ch. 46
•Monett Ch. 38
•Neosho Ch. 32
Poplar Bluff Ch. 39
Springfield Ch. 52
St. Charles Ch. 34

•ST. JOSEPH Ch. 16
St. Louis Ch. 18
MISSISSIPPI
Biloxi Ch. 29
•Bruce Ch. 7
•Calhoun City Ch. 34
Columbus Ch. 25
Grenada Ch. 25
•Jackson Ch. 64
McComb Ch. 36
Natchez Ch. 58
Pascagoula Ch. 46
MONTANA
•Billings Ch. 14
Great Falls Ch. 53
Helena Ch. 41
Kalispell Ch. 26
NORTH CAROLINA
Charlotte Ch. 68
•Charlotte/
Gastonia Ch. 62
Durham Ch. 56
Goldsboro Ch. 59
•GREENSBORO Ch. 61
Hendersonville Ch. 61
Raleigh Ch. 38
Statesville Ch. 66
Wilmington Ch. 20
NORTH DAKOTA
Fargo Ch. 56
Grand Forks Ch. 22
•Rugby Ch. 20
Williston Ch. 40
NEBRASKA
•Council Bluffs/
Lincoln Ch. 39
Ogallala Ch. 26
NEW JERSEY
Atlantic City Ch. 36
•Cape May/
Wildwood Ch. 5
NEW MEXICO
•Alamogordo Ch. 29
•ALBQUERQUE Ch. 23
•Carlsbad Ch. 63
•Clovis/Hobbs Ch. 65
Elida Ch 36
• Elida Ch. 36
•Farmington Ch. 47
•Hobbs Ch. 46
•Maljamar Ch. 46
Raton Ch. 18
•Roswell Ch. 27
•Ruidoso Ch. 45
NEVADA
Carson City Ch. 19
Las Vegas Ch. 57
Reno Ch. 45
NEW YORK
Albany Ch. 64
Binghampton Ch. 14
•BUFFALO Ch. 49

Glens Falls Ch. 14
Jamestown Ch. 10
•Massena Ch. 20
Olean Ch. 22
POUGHKEEPSIE Ch. 54
•Rochester Ch. 59
Utica Ch. 41
OHIO
CANTON Ch. 17
Chillicothe Ch. 40
•Columbus Ch. 24
Dayton Ch. 68
Kirkland/Cleveland Ch 51
•LEXINGTON Ch. 32
Lexington Ch. 32
•Marietta Ch. 26
•Marion Ch. 39
Portsmouth Ch. 21
•SANDUSKY Ch. 52
•Seaman Ch. 17
Springfield Ch. 47
•Toledo (North) Ch. 68
•Toledo (South) Ch. 46
Youngstown Ch. 39
Zanesville Ch. 36
OKLAHOMA
Ardmore Ch. 44
•Balko Ch. 25
•BARTLESVILE Ch. 17
•Elk City Ch. 52
•Guymon Ch. 53
Lawton Ch. 27
•Strong City Ch. 30
OKLAHOMA CTY Ch. 14
OREGON
Bend Ch. 33
Coos Bay Ch. 33
•Cottage Grove Ch. 50
•Eugene Ch. 59
Grants Pass Ch. 59
Klamath Falls Ch. 58
Lakeview Ch. 21
Medford Ch. 57
•PORTLAND Ch. 24
Roseburg Ch. 14
PENNSYLVANIA
Erie Ch. 44
•Kingston Ch. 54
Meadville Ch. 52
State College Ch. 42
Williamsport Ch. 11
SOUTH CAROLINA
•Anderson Ch. 18
Charleston Ch. 44
•GREENVILLE Ch. 16
•Greenville Ch. 58
Myrtle Beach Ch. 66
•Myrtle Beach Ch. 43
•Orangeburg Ch. 52
SOUTH DAKOTA
Aberdeen Ch. 20
Brookings Ch. 15

Huron Ch. 38
Madison Ch. 27
Rapid City Ch. 33
Sioux Falls Ch. 66
Yankton Ch. 31
TENNESSEE
Cookeville Ch. 46
Farragut Ch. 66
•Hendersonville Ch. 50
Jackson Ch. 35
•Memphis Ch. 65
•Memphis/Hly. Springs
  Ch. 40
Morristown Ch. 31
•Nashville Ch. 36
•Sharon Ch. 2
TEXAS
•Abilene Ch. 51
Austin Ch. 63
•BEAUMONT Ch. 34
Brownwood Ch. 26
College Station Ch. 57
DALLAS Ch. 58
Ft. Stockton/Apline Ch 30
•HARLINGEN Ch. 44
•HOUSTON Ch. 14
•Kerrville Ch. 2
•Killeen Ch. 31
Kingsville Ch. 47
•LeMesa Ch. 47
•Livingston Ch. 66
•Longview Ch. 10
•Lufkin Ch. 5
•Monahans Ch. 28
•ODESSA Ch. 42
Palestine Ch. 17
Paris Ch. 42
•Pecos Ch. 64
San Angelo Ch. 19
San Antonio Ch. 33
San Antonio Ch. 20
•Snyder Ch. 26
Texarkana Ch. 30
•Tyler Ch. 20
Victoria Ch. 43
•Wichita Falls Ch. 26
UTAH
Ogden Ch. 64
•Salt Lake City Ch. 36
Vernal Ch. 39
VIRGINIA
•Danville Ch. 18
Lynchburg Ch. 32
Roanoke Ch. 49
WASHINGTON
Aberdeen Ch. 23
Ellensburg Ch. 39
Longview Ch. 36
•Richland Ch. 49
SEATTLE/
TACOMA Ch. 20

Spokane Ch. 55
WENATCHEE CH 13
WENATCHEE CH 59
•Yakima Ch. 64
WISCONSIN
Green Bay Ch. 68
Janesville Ch. 19
•LaCross Ch. 44
Madison Ch. 33
Ripon Ch. 42
Sheboygan Ch. 20
Waupaca Ch. 55
WEST VIRGINIA
•Charleston Ch. 45
•Huntington Ch. 19
Parkersburg Ch. 39
WYOMING
•Casper Ch. 13
Green River Ch. 35

TBN RADIO STATIONS

KTBN SUPERPOWER
SHORTWAVE RADIO
8 A.M. - 6 P.M. (P.D.T.)
15.590 MHz.
6 P.M. - 8 A.M. (P.D.T.)
7.510 MHz.
(Reaching Around the
World)

RADIO PARADISE
ST. KITTS, WEST
INDIES
830 KHz. A.M.

HOQUIAM, WA
KGHO AM 1490
KGHO FM 95.3

**INTERNATIONAL
STATIONS**

NEVIS, W.I.
Charlestown Ch. 13
•GRAND CAYMAN IS.
Georgetown Ch. 21
•HAITI
Port-au-Prince Ch. 16
ST. LUCIA
Castries Ch. 13
•BELIZE
Belize City Ch. 13
•COSTA RICA
•San Jose Ch. 23
•Santa Elena Ch. 53
•Limon Ch. 23
•Cerro de la Muerte Ch. 53
Zapotal Ch 53
EL SALVADOR
San Salvador Ch. 25

•HONDURAS
•Tegulcigalpa Ch. 57
NICARAGUA
•Managua Ch. 21
•Esteli Ch. 25
•La Gateda Ch. 27
•ARGENTINA
•Buenos Aires Ch. 68
BRAZIL
Manaus Ch. 8
Portovelho Ch. 6
•BOLIVIA
• La Paz Ch. 27
CHILE
Valpariso Ch. 32
EQUADOR
Quito Ch. 27
Guayaquil Ch. 28
ITALY
Lombardia Region
Agno/Magnaso Ch. 39
Biella Ch. 59
Campione Ch. 44
Como Ch. 28
Ivrea Ch. 36
Maccagno Ch. 45
Milano Ch. 11
Novara Ch. 26
Pavia Certosa Ch. H1
Porto Ceresio Ch. 46
Valdosta Ch. 28
Varese Ch. 33
Viggiu Ch. 46
Piemonte Region
Torre Bert C. 60
Piazza Lancia Ch. 10
Pecetto Torino Ch. 27
LaMorra Ch. 60
Guarene Ch. 28
Azzano Ch. 29
St. Stefano Ch. 48
Mombaruzzo Ch. 68
Bricco Olio Ch. H2
Monte Ronzone Ch. 29
Corio Ch. 60
Nieve Ch. 42
Canale Ch. 26
Dogliana Ch. 21
Somano Ch. 42
Paroldo Ch. 42
Monchiero Ch. 42
St. Michele Mondovi Ch. 68
Alba Bricco Capre Ch 68
Lazio Region
Rome Ch. 33
Rome/Mt. Cavo Ch. 47
P. Nibbio Ch. 64
Mt. Calcarone Ch. 50
Mt. Artemisio Ch. 35
Rocca d'Arce Ch. 47
Fumone Ch. 39

Arpino Ch. 48
Valle Maio Ch. 61
Rocca Monfina Ch. 50
Mt. Orlando Ch. 48
Avezzano Ch. 31
Mt. Cicoli Ch. 42
Segni Ch. 34
Vicalvi Ch. 63
Montattico Ch. 53
Capistrello Ch. 29
Cavita d'Antino Ch. 63
Meta Ch. 58
Isola Liri Ch. 24
Subiaco Ch. 22
Gadamello Ch. 26
Mt. Amita Ch. 47
Mt. Paradiso Ch. 61
Scansano Ch. 54
Mt. St. Biagio Ch. 57
St. di Fondi Ch. 24
St. Felice Circeo Ch. 43
Secca Volsci Ch. 49
St. Vito Romano Ch. 44
Castro Vollsci Ch. 31
St. Incarico Ch. 41

Itri Ch. 224
Balsorano Ch. 35
Pesche Ch. 58
PHILIPINES
Manila
Tonga
Nukyu-Alofa Ch. 7
NEW ZEALAND
SWITZERLAND
Locarno Ch. 37
Lugano/Campione Ch. 44
GREECE
Athens Ch. 62
Corinth Ch. 54
Macedonia Ch. 62
•**ALBANIA (gov't. owned)**
•**ICELAND**
•Reykjavik Ch. 45 & 53
RUSSIA
St. Petersburg Ch. 40
CISKEI, S. AFRICA
Bisho Ch. 24

TRANSKEI, S. AFRICA
Umtata Ch. 67
Butterworth Ch. 25
Ngangelizwe Ch. 67
Mt. Ayliff Ch. 27
Queenstown Ch 10
Port St. Johns (under const.)
Engcobo (under const.)
Mt. Fletcher (under const.)
•**ZAMBIA**
•Lusaka
•**SWAZILAND**
•Mbabane
•**NAMIBIA**

•Windhoek
•**LESOTHO**
•Maseru
•**BOPHUTHATSWANA**
•**ZAIRE**
•Kinshasa
•**REPUBLIC OF SOUTH AFRICA**
•TV 1 - Ch. 13
•TV 2 - Ch. 9

For More Information, Please Write:

Trinity Broadcasting Network

Post Office Box A
Santa Ana, CA 92711
24 Hour Prayer Line: (714) 731-1000

I WANT TO HELP YOU WIN YOUR WAR ON DEBT!

It has taken a year of hard work and now all of the material for the Debt Free Army is ready to be placed in your hands.

Enlist Today And The Following Materials Will Be Immediately Sent To You:

YOUR PERSONAL ONE-OF-A KIND BATTLE PLAN PORTFOLIO WHICH INCLUDES:

A large 12-place, library-style audio cassette binder. •Your Battle Plan Notebook with 12 full-color dividers designed to index over 250 pages of Debt-Free Strategies. •"The First Thirty Days To Victory" - a comprehensive "Master Plan" designed to help you become debt free. •The Debt Free Army Ammunition. (Your first monthly audio tape of insight, inspiration, and motivation.) This is a personal one-on-one tape you will receive from Brother John each month.